BRITISH
PHRASEBOOK

Dr Elizabeth Bartsch-Parker
Stephen Burgen
Richard Crowe
Dr Roibeard O Maolalaigh
Dr Dominic Watt

British phrasebook
1st edition – June 1999

Published by
Lonely Planet Publications Pty Ltd ABN 36 005 607 983
90 Maribyrnong St, Footscray, Victoria 3011, Australia

Lonely Planet Offices
Australia Locked Bag 1, Footscray, Victoria 3011
USA 150 Linden St, Oakland CA 94607
UK 72-82 Rosebery Ave, London, EC1R 4RW
France 1 rue du Dahomey, 75011 Paris

Cover illustration
At the Boozer by Mic Looby

ISBN 0 86442 484 1

About the Authors

428

B 77

Dr Elizabeth Bartsch-Parker wrote the British English section. She is a native of Milwaukee, Wisconsin and received her PhD from the University of Wisconsin at Milwaukee. Her dissertation was on Thomas Hardy. She lectured in English at the UW-M, the University of Giessen in Germany and has taught A-level English in England. Dr Bartsch-Parker has three children, and resides in England with her British husband.

Stephen Burgen wrote the introduction, A Short History of English. He is a journalist on *The Times* in London and is the author of *Your Mother's Tongue*, a comparative study of insults and invective in 21 European tongues, published by Gollancz.

Richard Crowe, author of the chapter on Welsh, lives in Aberystwyth and works for the University of Wales on the *Dictionary of the Welsh Language* – the authoritative historical dictionary of Welsh. He has also taught Welsh as a second language to adults at the Department of Continuing Education. In his spare time he writes poetry and short stories.

Rob O Maolalaigh authored the Scottish Gaelic section. He was born in Dublin where he studied Irish Gaelic and mathematics at University College, Dublin. In his early 20s he moved to Scotland, where with his knowledge of Irish Gaelic, he gradually made the transition to Scottish Gaelic. He completed a doctoral thesis on aspects of the historical development of the Gaelic languages at the University of Edinburgh, where he now lectures on Irish Gaelic and Scottish Gaelic in the Department of Celtic. He is the author of the teach-yourself book *Scottish Gaelic in Three Months*.

Dr Dominic Watt wrote the chapters on Accents & Dialects and Cockney. He is Research Fellow in the Department of Linguistics and Phonetics, University of Leeds, where he's researching language acquisition. His research interests include phonetics, phonology, and linguistic variation and change.

From the Authors

Elizabeth Bartsch-Parker would like to express her loving gratitude to her dad, who inspired in her since childhood a fascination for words and wordplay, and to her late father-in-law, Jack Parker, who never tired of discussing British terms and phrases, with all their nuances, with her in his perspicacious and good-humoured manner. She also owes thanks to her mother-in-law Pat Parker, and her children, Chip, Jeff and Janet for all their support and enthusiastic interest in this project. Most of all, she thanks her husband, Chris, for his utterly invaluable advice and for his patient assistance as she worked up and emailed off to her editors her part in this book on her intransigent computer. Finally, she thanks the writers and compilers of the *OED*, beginning with the 'professor and madman', for providing that resource to people like her, who would be lost without it.

Richard Crowe would like to thank all his email correspondents who helped with certain aspects of the chapter, and especially Owen Thomas for his encyclopaedic knowledge of swear words.

Dominic Watt would like to thank the following people for their helpful input and suggestions – Carmen Llamas, Paul Foulkes, Bethan Davies, Diane Nelson, Victoria Cumming, Mark Jones, Louise Mullany, Anna Churchill, Will Allen, Lyndsay Jarvis, Julie Watt, Louise Cunningham and Jane Stuart-Smith.

From the Publisher

Many people had a hand in producing this book. Sally Steward and Peter D'Onghia instigated and guided the project. Vicki Webb edited the book, Olivier Breton helped with editing and Dom Watt and Liz Filleul had a butcher's at the manuscript and made many valuable suggestions. Joanne Adams and Brendan Dempsey designed and laid out the book with their (un)usual flair. Thanks to Mic Looby for his bobbydazzler of a cover, Julian Chapple for his class illustrations and Jim Miller for producing the top maps. Quentin 'Ginger' Frayne provided many excellent brews.

Martin Hughes wrote the sections on music and sport, with contributions from Elizabeth Bartsch-Parker. Doug McKinlay contributed his considerable expertise on pubs. Thanks to Mark Newbrook and Jane Curtain for their contribution to sections of the Sports chapter.

CONTENTS

INTRODUCTION

A SHORT HISTORY OF ENGLISH 11

Introduction 11
Recycled Words 14
Invasions 15
A Layered language 17
Borrowing 19
Wordplay 20
A Simplified Structure 23
Spelling 27
'Good' English 28
The Spread of English 31
Abbreviations 34

BRITISH ENGLISH

PRONUNCIATION 37

Placenames 39

MEETING PEOPLE 43

Greetings 43
People & Occupations 45
Children 46
Telephone Talk 47

SLANG & COMMON EXPRESSIONS 49

Slang 49
Common Expressions 55
Brand Names..................... 62

COCKNEY 65

GETTING AROUND 71

Train 71
Taxi 73
Buses 73
Car 74
Bicycle 78

ACCOMMODATION 79

Housing 80
Around the House 81

AROUND TOWN 83

IN THE COUNTRY 91

FOOD & DRINK 95

Food 95   Drinks 103

ENTERTAINMENT 111

Shopping 111   Festivals 121
Theatre 116   Useful Terms 122
Music 119

SPORT 125

Football 125   Cricket 138
Rugby Union 135   Other Sports
Rugby League 138   & Games 143

BRITISH SOCIETY 147

Government & Politics 147   Titles & Forms
Education 152   of Address 156

AMERICAN – BRITISH 159

Spelling 159   British Words 164
Terms & Phrases 161

ABBREVIATIONS & ACRONYMS 179

REGIONAL LANGUAGE

ACCENTS & DIALECTS 183

London & The   The North-East of
    South-East 186   England 194
The Mid-North of England: North Of The Border:
    Yorkshire 189   Scotland 199

The North-West
    of England 207
Wales 212
The West Midlands 215

The South-West
    of England 219
Slang 223

SCOTTISH GAELIC 229

Introduction 229
Transliterations 231
Pronunciation 233
Grammar 236
Meeting People 245

Around Town 252
Food & Drink 255
Time, Dates
    & Festivals 258
Numbers 261

WELSH 263

Introduction 263
Pronunciation 264
Grammar 266
Meeting People 273
Going Out 280

Food & Drink 283
Placenames 285
Time, Dates
    & Festivals 286
Numbers 288

SUGGESTED READING 291

INDEX 297

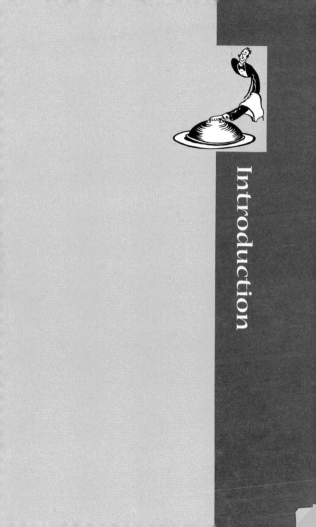

Introduction

A SHORT HISTORY
OF ENGLISH

INTRODUCTION

The English – in England – are among the most tolerant bigots on Earth. Once they leave their shores the tolerant half of the equation tends to go out the window, but at home they've absorbed invaders and immigrants for 2000 years with unusual nonchalance. There's no doubt they're racist, but there's nothing like the Ku Klux Klan in England and far right politics has never occupied anything but a largely irrelevant fringe. There's anti-Semitism, too, but there hasn't been a pogrom since 1290, which few of their European neighbours can boast. The English are accommodating – it's one of their great strengths. They don't care where things come from; if they want them they take them and make them their own. These days curry, not fish and chips or roast beef, is the national dish.

The English language is the same. In the 1500 years of its existence, English has been defined by two characteristics – openness to other languages and a drive towards simplification. English is a magpie tongue, borrowing unselfconsciously from the world's vocabulary – even when a word of the same meaning already exists – always on the lookout for some new shade of meaning. And yet it remains resolutely and unmistakably itself. This willingness to borrow and a hunger for synonyms has been a feature of the language since the 5th century, when the Anglo-Saxons were invited over to sort out the warring tribes at the end of the Roman occupation. The Romans had made little impact on what was then the national language, Cymric, the antecedent of Welsh, spoken by King Arthur. The native tongues of Italy, France and the Iberian peninsula disappeared altogether under the Romans, to be replaced by what have become Italian, French, Spanish, Catalan and Portuguese. The only indigenous language that survived was the Basque tongue, Euskera. On the other hand, when the Romans abandoned Britain after a 450-year occupation – typically the British didn't drive them out, but waited for them to leave – they left behind fewer than 10 words of Latin origin (the thousands of Latin-based words that now form part of the language began to be introduced with the arrival of St Augustine in 597AD and the subsequent spread of Christianity).

Of all the invaders, only the Romans left. The Anglo-Saxons drove the Celts into the hills and stayed; the Vikings conquered and were then absorbed; the Normans – French-speaking Vikings – were largely ignored. These events affected but didn't eradicate the language, which remained very much itself. As English probably contains more loanwords than any other language, this may seem a contradiction, but it is precisely its self-confidence that has allowed it to borrow with such *sans souci*. There's no English equivalent of the Académie française, standing like some immigration officer at the gates of pure French in a forlorn attempt to keep the foreigners out. As far as the English language is concerned, all foreigners are welcome, quite the opposite of German, from which – although it's a close relative of Anglo-Saxon – it has borrowed the least (hinterland, angst, blitz, zeitgeist, hamster, poodle). German itself resists loanwords, insisting on filling the need for new words through the forced marriage of existing German ones. For example, when the rise of modern science demanded a new vocabulary, English and the Romance languages tipped their hats to Rome and the ancient Greeks and shaped their concepts to fit modern needs. Hence the word hydrogen, for instance. But this is anathema to German, which had to make up its own inelegant word, *Wasserstoff* 'water stuff' to fill the gap. Today science and technology accounts for more than half the English vocabulary, most of it concocted from Ancient Greek and Latin.

From the earliest records English has shown this hunger for new words and has been cavalier about where it gets them. In the epic *Beowulf*, thought to be written in the 8th century and one of the earliest surviving English texts, there are 17 different expressions for the sea and 11 for a ship. Perhaps this is only to be expected from a seafaring nation, but even this wasn't enough. Dutch had to be raided to give us yacht, cruise, deck, keelhaul and freebooter and then we had to go to Spain for galleon and armada, France for frigate and buccaneer and Tamil Nadu for catamaran. The language of love has also spread its net wide. Love itself, along with kiss and handsome and pretty, are all of Anglo-Saxon origin. But sex, beauty, gorgeous, court, embrace and romance have all come to us from the French. Flirting is of unknown origin but petting we learnt from Scottish Gaelic and both seduction and, perhaps carelessly, pregnancy, we got from the Latin.

In English the most simple concepts surround themselves with an entourage of synonyms,

RUBBER

In Britain, a rubber is something you erase pencil marks with, and is therefore of little use for avoiding sexually-transmitted diseases.

gathered from who cares where. Take the ways of describing the coming together of two or more people. This could take the form of a meeting or gathering (Old English), assignation or encounter (both Old French), rendezvous, rally or reunion (French), caucus (Algonquin), pow-wow (Narragansett) or a tryst (Old French). All of these words have essentially the same meaning but together they provide scope for enormous nuance. No native English speaker would confuse the romantic sub-text of a tryst with the political implications of a caucus.

On the other hand this yearning for synonyms could just as well be viewed negatively as a legacy of the German obsession

HISTORY

with precision. Do we need so many words? The word *pista*, for example, in both Italian and Spanish means variously a small path, tennis court, runway, dance floor, racecourse, athletics track, ski run, ice rink and bowling alley. Evidently they're confident that context will make clear just which *pista* is which.

RECYCLED WORDS

Words don't stand still and some have gone through a perplexing and often inexplicable evolution. Take that overworked little word nice. It derives from the Latin *nescius*, meaning ignorant. Since the Middle Ages it has stood for: foolish, wanton, ostentatious, neat, refined, strange, effeminate, coy, hard to please, obscure, exact, risky, deft, pleasant and agreeable. Pretty nice work from one little word. Pretty itself has meant, since its first appearance in Old English: capricious, overbearing, clever, roguish, humorous and, well, pretty. All this to arrive at the vacuous standby, pretty nice, which as far as really meaning anything goes, is pretty much of a muchness.

The longer a word stays in the language, the more changes it seems destined to go through. Take gossip. In Old English a gossip was a godfather or mother (from god-sibb); in Middle English it was a close friend; in the 16th century a gossip was a woman friend invited to be present at a birth and some time in the 19th century it acquired its current meaning. Some words even change sex – a punk was a female then a male prostitute and harlots were male until the late Middle Ages.

Words also fall victim to fashion – the word boom
for instance. Up until the 1980s recession, boom was a good word.
It meant jobs and money and a two-car garage. But then it
got tainted by bust, its ugly sister, and the new fiscal pieties have
denounced boom as a dirty word. Boom is bad, what used to
be a boom is now an overheated economy. And whatever
happened to the Lumpenproletariat, the term coined by Marx
out of the German for rags and Latin for the lowest class of
citizen? Sometime in the 1980s the Lumpenproletariat was
supplanted by the equally ill-starred underclass, this time an
English-Latin composite.

INVASIONS

Of course not all of this borrowing of other people's words has
been entirely voluntary, so we should briefly survey the impact on
English of the Viking and Norman invasions. It appears that
unfavourable climatic changes in the 8th century drove the
previously peaceable Scandinavian shepherds to turn their backs
on their flocks, jump into boats and spend the next two hundred
years laying waste to northern Europe. They asserted their
authority over much of Britain and Ireland with exceptional
violence, even for those times. Their presence lives on in English
placenames, as in places ending in -by (farm) such as Grimsby or
Derby; -thorp (village) as in Althorp; -thwaite (a cleared piece of
land) as in Braithwaite; or -toft (piece of ground) as in Lowestoft.

After a few centuries the Norsemen seemed to lose interest or,
at the very least, were absorbed into the Anglo-Saxon body
politic. In the meantime they introduced perhaps 900 new words,
including such stalwarts as husband, window, egg, law, take,
knife, root, sly, dregs and surnames ending in -son. They also
passed on a bit of grammar in the form of they, them and their.
Old English already had a home, the Norsemen gave us a house,
but as they shared the same gods as the Anglo-Saxons, the days of

the weeks remained unaffected, named after Saturn, the Sun and Moon, and the gods Tiw, Woden, Thor and Freya. The further north you go in the British Isles, the more words of Norse origin survive. In the Shetland Islands as many as 1500 Old Norse words remain in use.

The French Connection

The Norman Conquest of 1066 was the equivalent of Israel's Six Day War – it was all over before you could blink. For the next 300 years, the official language was French but it affected as little as 20% of the population while the rest went on speaking English. It was probably during this period, when kings, clerics and scholars took little interest in the English language and its development was left in the hands of the common people, that the process of simplifying and stripping down the grammar began to accelerate. Nevertheless, as many as 10,000 English words arrived directly from Norman French. A significant proportion of the language of government and jurisprudence derives from the Norman conquest: court, parliament, tyrant, justice, sovereign, adultery and marriage among them.

In later centuries we helped ourselves to the rich store of French words devised to express class distinction, among them bourgeois, arriviste, parvenu, nouveau riche, elite, faux pas, chauvinism, limousine and chauffeur. The word snobbery itself is English, of course. No one has ever accused the English of being chic, and they've had to ransack French bon mots in order to acquire some élan and panache, a blasé veneer of je ne sais quoi to cover their confusion over what is in vogue and what passé – anything to pass themselves off as sophisticated. Now there's a word with a track record. Starting off from the Greek *sophisma*, meaning a trick or clever device, it then described the school of philosophy that employed a plausible but ultimately fallacious line of argument to prove its case. It went on to mean adulterate, especially wine with water or gold with base metal, and acquired its current meaning in America early this century.

It's estimated that 4300 words of Old English survived the Viking and Norman conquests but these words are so basic – God, man, woman, child, love, drink, live, go, at, to, for – that they make up most of everyday speech. It's claimed that the 100 most commonly used words are all of Anglo-Saxon origin. Take something fundamental like a door. All but two of the following associated words – frame, jamb, ajar, lock, key, panel, architrave, open, ajar, close, knob, handle, sill and hinge – are Old or Middle English. Jamb is from French and architrave Italian.

A LAYERED LANGUAGE

For the essentials of life, English always offers a choice between a simple Anglo-Saxon word and a fancy one, usually derived from Latin or Greek. You can believe in werewolves (Old English) or lycanthropes (Greek). You can choose to make (Old English) something, or if that's too easy, there's always the option to manufacture (Latin via Italian), fabricate or construct (Latin) or synthesise (Greek). You can talk or chat (Middle English) or, if you want to be taken more seriously, communicate and converse (Latin). There are also many instances where an Anglo-Saxon noun turns Latin when it becomes an adjective – earth and terrestrial, horse and equestrian. The Latin words aren't necessarily better (an onanist is still a wanker, after all) but it's striking that whenever people feel that what they have to say is important – giving evidence in court, for example, or faced with a TV camera – they dive headlong into words and constructions of Latin and Greek origin, usually at the expense of clarity. This is especially true of Americans. It's curious that the nation that gave us the sound-bite and snappy dialogue also wallows in such grotesque constructions as 'in the current time-frame' when they want to say 'now' and produces newspapers of such merciless turgidity as the *New York Times* and *Washington Post*.

On the other hand English is so reducible it has been possible to produce an entire sub-language in the form of tabloid journalism. It's doubtful that other languages could produce a headline as succinct as the *New York Post's* Headless body found in topless bar or could devise the bizarre British tabloid shorthand of:

> love rats, porn kings, tug of love babies and fun-loving blonde mother-of-two in kinky sex romp with sex-change vicar.

Not to mention the tortured puns such as Would Hugh believe it? when actor Hugh Grant was caught with a prostitute or From toe job to no job on the resignation of a government minister with a known foot fetish.

BORROWING

No one has bothered to invade Britain since 1066, so in order to extend their vocabulary the English had to go out and conquer the world, otherwise they wouldn't now be sitting in their pyjamas (Urdu) smoking hashish (Arabic) – from which, via the French *hachichien*, we've derived assassin – doing origami (Japanese). For 800 years, after Strongbow invaded Ireland in 1171, the English plundered the riches of the world, and among those riches were words. Some, such as billabong, have remained where they found them and become part of the English implanted by the colonisers, while thousands of others – slogan (Gaelic), thug (Hindi), potato (Spanish) intelligentsia (Russian), sauna (Finnish), anorak (Inuit), tycoon (Japanese), taboo (Tongan), cosy (Scots) – have entered the English mainstream. Just as it has borrowed almost the entire French vocabulary of haute couture, for the finer points of architecture it has turned to Italian – cupola, capital, mezzanine, portico, corridor, dome – while sticking to Anglo-Saxon for the basics (wall, window, door, brick, roof). Italian has also made a sizeable contribution to the language of war and one, colonel, exemplifies the apparently random and cavalier approach English takes to the pronunciation of foreign imports. Colonel came to us somewhat indirectly from the Italian *colonello*, meaning a column of troops. So why, when pronouncing colonel phonetically doesn't present a problem to the English palate, make it sound the same as the stone inside a fruit? Why do we give rendezvous and parquet correct French pronunciation, but not repartee? And how is it that Americans say repartee correctly (*repart-ay*) and yet pronounce route like rout?

There is also little discernible pattern in the way English sometimes imports a word such as guitar or marijuana (both Spanish) without alteration and pronounces them correctly, and when it deems it necessary to anglicise, as with cockroach and crocodile, from the Spanish *cucaracha* and *cocodrilo*. Sometimes

HISTORY

we can't decide. Even on the BBC, the word junta is pronounced either with the first syllable sounding like the *ju-* in 'junk' or correctly as *hunta*, depending on who's reading the news. Now in the global village new words rush in within a matter of weeks, whenever there's some upheaval in a foreign land. First they refer only to the place they came from – samizdat, glasnost, perestroika – but soon they enter the language in their own right and it isn't long before you hear someone say something like, 'It's time there was a little more glasnost in the Ministry of Trade'. The recent gifts from Islam – jihad, fatwa, and intifada – are already being adapted for domestic consumption.

To the question, 'How many words do you need?', English replies, 'How many have you got?'. It never seems to have enough. About 50 years ago, linguists produced Basic English, a stripped down version with a vocabulary of 850 words. There's nothing you can't say in Basic English, but so what, if there's little that can be said well. The question is, did we know we suffered from existential angst before we had the words, or has the condition been spread by the words? There's no Italian word for angst, from which we might conclude that it's not something they suffer from. But then Italian has no word for womaniser either, and there are plenty of those. In Spanish, there's no word that means self-indulgent, and if you want to say the water is shallow, you say *no es profundo*, it's not deep. That's fine, it conveys the necessary information. But without shallow you lose out on metaphor and deprive whoever it was who said it of the chance to say that President Ford was 'so shallow you could wade through his deepest thoughts and not get your ankles wet'.

WORDPLAY

English loves wordplay, and appears to have done so pretty well from the start. Chaucer certainly liked it, not to mention Shakespeare, who alone is credited with adding 2000 words to the language in addition to hundreds of everyday idioms –

poisoned chalice, one fell swoop, foul play, in my mind's eye, cold comfort, cruel to be kind – which have remained in use for 400 years. At much the same time, many expressions entered the language from the Authorised Version of the Bible, usually known as the King James Bible, and are still with us today – salt of the earth, sour grapes, skin of your teeth, suffer fools gladly.

HISTORY

Metaphorically Speaking

To play on words you need a sense of metaphor, and there's nothing the English language likes more than metaphor – it's metaphor mad. Every industry, every sport, every form of endeavour generates its own vocabulary. Most remain within the confines of the activity in question, but as soon as they overlap with the culture at large, English mines them for metaphors. Take the military and naval spheres. Before you even start to drum up support for your campaign, you must nail your colours to the mast and set your sights on a united front, steering clear of loose cannons, camp followers and anyone likely to break ranks under their baptism of fire, and recruit only those who'll stick to their guns, even if they get caught in the crossfire in no-man's land. And that's only a start, there are dozens more.

As England has been continuously at war with someone or other for hundreds of years, this is perhaps not so surprising. On the other hand, very few of us have ever stepped into the ring and yet all of us have from time to time found ourselves on the ropes, talking a good fight but unable to box clever and forced to slug it out toe-to-toe with some heavyweight who doesn't pull their punches. You have to learn to take the body blows and roll with the punches and not hope to be saved by the bell, because if you can't punch your weight you'll get caught by the old one-two and you'll be out for the count. It's either that or take a dive or throw in the towel.

Any number of activities have been trawled for metaphors. Hunting has given us sitting duck, stalking horse, cut to the chase, open season and beating about the bush. From animal life we've taken bitch and cow, penguin suit, a game of cat and mouse, stubborn as a mule, water off a duck's back, snake in the grass and so on. Even flowers have supplied us with pansy, wallflower, shrinking violet and lily-livered. The English appetite for metaphor appears insatiable.

DID YOU KNOW ... When Edward I's wife Eleanor died in 1290, the grief-stricken king ordered memorial crosses to be placed wherever her body passed the night on its way from Nottinghamshire to London, for burial in Westminster Abbey. Of these 12 crosses, only three originals survive. A Victorian reproduction stands in the courtyard at Charing Cross station (Charing is an anglicisation of *Chère Reine*, 'dear queen').

HISTORY

A SIMPLIFIED STRUCTURE

The tendency of the English language to borrow from other tongues reflects and has perhaps encouraged a certain lawlessness in regard to structure. English grammar is rather like the British Constitution – there's a general idea of the rights and wrongs, but the fact is that neither can properly be said to exist. (Or, neither can be said properly to exist – which some would insist is the more correct syntax.) While on the one hand ceaselessly expanding its vocabulary, English has exhibited a consistent and ingenious urge towards simplification, stripping down the engine of language to as few basic components as possible. Old English was, as many modern languages still are, inflected. In inflected tongues, words change their form not only according to tense but according to their function, the relationship between the person speaking and the person addressed, gender and so on.

Old English had – like modern German – three genders. Nouns had numerous cases and adjectives had as many as 11 forms. By the end of the 14th century, English had wisely dumped cases, genders and most of the other encumbrances of inflection. It disposed of cases by employing a range of little words to express the relationship between, say, the subject and the object. In an inflected language, word endings have to change in order to clarify how the word stands in relation to others in a sentence. English solved this problem by leaving the word alone and using simple prepositions – to, with, from, at, in and so on – to express relation. Many other tongues, the Romance languages for example, use the same device. They, however, cling to the idea of gender, which in English was already heading for the grammatical dustbin by Chaucer's time. And good riddance, too. It's useful to distinguish between a man and a woman, a cow and a bull, but can there really be any sustainable argument for allocating a gender to objects and activities that have no sexual characteristics? Does it add anything to a language to give a crankshaft or an omelette a gender? Even where there is some logic, say, in Mother

Earth being feminine, why should the equally abundant sea be masculine? Or why in Spanish, for example, is the fruit of a tree invariably feminine when the tree that bears it surely a definitively female activity – is masculine? The English language considered the evidence in favour of gender and delivered its verdict – case dismissed.

Despite its love of synonyms, English often dispenses with linguistic niceties when it feels no useful distinction is being made and when there's little danger of the listener getting the wrong message. For example, French and Spanish both feel it necessary to distinguish between knowing in the sense of acquaintance – I know *(connaître/conocer)* Charlie very well – and knowing in the sense of knowledge – I know *(savoir/saber)* how to play the piano. English is content with the one verb. Likewise both languages are loath to confuse the temporary and immutable facts of existence. So in French you say I am *(être)* a woman and I have *(avoir)* hunger or in Spanish, I am *(ser)* from Madrid but I am *(estar)* in Valencia. In English, we consider such distinctions unnecessary and don't imagine that by saying 'I'm thirsty' that anyone is going to imagine that the speaker is the personification of thirst.

However, in common with Romance and other languages, English does feel a need to distinguish between hearing and listening, looking and seeing, and knowing and believing. English has an ambivalent attitude to reflexive verbs, those verbs which refer to things we do to ourselves, such as wash and get out of bed. Many other languages consider it necessary to insert the word 'myself' when using such verbs like in French *Je me lave*, literally 'I wash myself'. English sort of does this but only in the present tense when the act is actually in progress. Here, instead of saying 'I shave', we use the form 'I am shaving'. But once it's done – I shaved this morning – there's no sense of it being reflexive.

A Versatile Language

One of the ingenuities of English is to let the same word do service as a noun or a verb (push, drink, love, smoke) and to make simple compounds (handbook, doorknob, coathanger, breastfeed). However, it eschews the unwieldy compounds of several nouns typical of the way in which German creates German conglomerate words – *Gewerkschaftsbewegung*, 'trade union movement' – rather than import a simpler one from outside. Sometimes English resists such conversions. For example, access, formerly used only as a noun, has reluctantly been granted the status of a verb thanks mainly to the prevalence of computers and the need to access electronic files.

Another of its clever tricks is to employ an army of prefixes and suffixes to alter the sense of a word. Vast numbers of words are constructed through the addition of a simple in-, un-, re-, dis-, pre-, -y, -ible, -ably, -ness and so forth. Likewise, negation can be expressed through the application of a-, anti-, ir-, non-, in-, il-, un- and so on. It is also very economical in its use of articles – in English you can say 'I'm going to bed' or 'I don't want lunch' or 'It's Derby day', where other languages would require articles (the bed, the lunch, the day of the Derby). Plurals, too, are simplified in most cases to the addition of an s, although a few Old English forms remain, such as children, men, women and feet. And then there are the odd ones out – fish, sheep, deer – which seem to be there for no other reason than to make foreigners look stupid when they say 'sheeps'.

A further advance was made through the democratisation of forms of address. In German, there are seven forms of the word 'you' – in Romance languages there's still considerable anxiety and confusion over when to use the informal and formal forms of you, expressed in French as *tu* and *vous*. In English, you don't have to worry about how you stand in relation to someone else or what degree of respect they should be shown because everyone is simply you. The only other forms of address occur in the sort of formal settings where anachronisms are cherished, such as parliament (**Madam Speaker, the Right Honourable Gentleman**) or courtrooms (**milud, Your Worship**).

But in its drive towards simplification, probably its greatest achievement was the invention of the phrasal verb. These combinations of little words (basically in the form of verb + preposition or adverb = new meaning) form the basis of everyday speech and are the key to the structural simplicity of the language. They're also the bane of foreign students learning English, firstly because there are so many of them and secondly because they have to be learned by heart. There's no way a student of the language could deduce that you **get on** and **get off** a train, boat or plane but **get in** and **get out** of a car. Phrasal verbs, if English isn't your mother tongue, will drive you crazy.

Take the word **get**, an Old English survivor meaning variously to obtain, beget, guess and forget. **Get** is a little monster – **get, got, gotten**, the latter forbidden in England but widespread in America (although **forgotten** is fine on both sides of the water). But **get** has only a part-time job meaning to obtain – it spends the rest of its life joined to other words in order to create a new meaning. **Get** is the grammatical equivalent of an action hero, it's everywhere. Right from the **get go**, when you **get up** and **get out** of bed and remember you **got out** of your head last night again which is **getting** to be a drag because it makes **getting** started so hard when you can hardly **get on** your **get up** and **get out** of the house. And that's before you **get** the bus to work and the boss who you don't get along with gets on your case, he just doesn't get it that you've got a life, but he gets over it and you get on with it and the day gets better, you get by at least, even if all you think about is getting out of there.

What a brilliantly simple little device, but what a nightmare for the non-native speaker. There are hundreds of others. Think of what is done with make – 'I couldn't make out why he would make off with my make-up but rather than make a scene I made my mind up not to make anything of it'. And it's not just the verbs. Take the little words up and down. You can look them up, read up on them, write them up and write them down. It's up to you. It's certainly not down to me. If you can master the phrasal verbs, you can speak English. Not very beautifully, perhaps, but it will be English very much as it is spoken.

A problem with learning English is if you try to guess, say, the adjectival form of a noun, you can never be sure of getting it right. Take the following:

clamour	clamorous
glamour	glamorous
humour	humorous

OK, you see the pattern, but then look what happens:

splendour	splendid
favour	favourite
colour	colourful
savour	savoury (which is both noun and adjective)

SPELLING

Anyone attempting to learn English would be well advised to listen but not to attempt to read because there are few languages with such an eccentric, not to say perverse, approach to spelling. English spelling is so illogical and bears so little relation to pronunciation that even well-educated native speakers are often poor spellers. Take the triptych siege, seize and beige. Or the different pronunciations of rough, cough, through, though and bough. Or what price a discount Viscount? Part of the problem is that it's such a mongrel tongue and over the years it has, if anything, got worse. In Middle English a debt was written dette, for example. Attempts to rationalise English spelling have been passionately resisted. Even now, people in Britain rail against the eminently sensible American decision to drop the 'u' from words such as colour and glamour. Indeed, there's nothing like an innocent Americanism to make an English person turn purple. They hate it that Americans say 'he took it in stride' rather than 'in his stride', or the construction 'I'll write you as soon as I get there' even though the English are perfectly happy with 'I'll phone you'. Another pet hate is 'she won't commit' as an alternative to the more reflexive 'she won't commit herself'.

'GOOD' ENGLISH

English as it's spoken – and written too – and how it should be spoken is the source of endless and mostly futile debate. As we've seen, during the 300 years that the ruling class spoke French, the lower orders were stripping English of its airs and graces until they'd made it something they felt at home in. The result was a language with hardly a semblance of what could properly be called grammar. And so it continued until the 18th century when some scholars decided they'd devise rules to make English conform to the rules of Latin grammar, that is, to a language with inflections, genders, cases and all the other baggage that English had so blithely dispensed with.

We're still living with the results of this idiotic exercise, roughly on a par with playing the piano with your feet, in that it can be done after a fashion, but so what? It's thanks to this foolishness that you're not supposed to end a sentence with a preposition – a rule which Winston Churchill dismissed with the comment 'this is the sort of nonsense up with which I will not put' – use a double negative or split an infinitive. There was uproar in 1998 when the *Oxford English Dictionary* became the last of the major dictionaries to declare that one might split an infinitive without risking eternal damnation in syntactic hell. Not everyone agreed. *The Times* declaimed, 'If a verb needs an adverb, goes the maxim, it is the wrong verb. If it needs the extra crutch of the adverb located within its infinitive, the poor thing must be on its knees and begging for help. A split infinitive is a boy sent on a man's errand. Avoid it. The case for change is not proven'.

Nevertheless, barely a month later, *The Guardian* began its page one lead with the sentence, 'Iran is preparing to formally and publicly withdraw its support for the fatwa on Salman Rushdie ...' – a double split infinitive, no less. It was always the case that these rules could be broken if you held a poetic licence, however, which is why, when an editor corrected a split infinitive in a manuscript, Raymond Chandler retorted, 'When I split an infinitive, sir, it stays split'.

Campaigns for good English have a long pedigree. Jonathan Swift were among many who – surprisingly for writers – wanted the language fixed and protected from foreign imports. The mailbags of the BBC and newspapers such as *The Times* are stuffed with outraged letters complaining about the desecration of the language in some report, usually in the form of a misplaced gerund, the use of 'who' instead of 'whom', or the incorrect use of a verb beside a collective noun. This in itself is a peculiarity. English grammar insists that a collection of things or persons, such as IBM or the government, is singular and therefore you must say, the government is, not the government are. But even this is inconsistent. The army is but the police are. Australia as a country is, but Australia the cricket team are. Even the BBC, seen by many as a bastion of good English, constantly breaks this rule.

There is, of course, a need for Standard English, which since the 18th century has centred on London. Every written language needs some agreed standard to bind its many dialects, rather in the way modern Standard Italian – which has existed for little more than a century – forms a bridge between the dozens of dialects most Italians speak at home. In terms of accent, Received Pronunciation (RP) is only spoken by the middle and upper classes of the southeast of England and those educated in public (private) schools. It's not necessarily the easiest form to understand. In the case of the upper class, it's sometimes almost impossible to understand at all. As RP is the form most used in language teaching, it's now spoken by more foreigners than native speakers. Accent aside, most people don't speak what is considered 'good' English. They use double negatives (He don't never answer; I ain't got none) non-standard parts of verbs (She don't care; Oh yes she do) or non-standard pronouns (That's alright for he; That's not for we; Us'll see about that; Whatever he dos, it won't be to I). There's also recently been an increase in the use of interrogative forms in what are statements, not questions.

> 'Where are you going?'
>
> 'I'm going to the shops, innit.'

This has become even more pronounced by the growing tendency to end statements with an upward inflection, making every statement sound like a question. This habit, formerly rare in southern England, has become a defining characteristic of what has become known as Estuary English and is thought to have been reinforced via the popularity of Australian soap operas such as *Neighbours* and *Home and Away*. A rising inflection is common in both Australian and New Zealand English.

Estuary English, so called because it's a sort of sub-Cockney spread along the Thames estuary in the post-war London diaspora, is fast becoming the new standard English, to the despair – naturally – of the adherents of RP. Its chief features are rising inflection, constant use of innit, a glottal t rendering the double 't' in butter almost silent and making 'alright' sound like *orwhy* and, in general, a slack-jawed, floppy-tongued way of speaking that knocks the corners off consonants and lets the vowels whine to themselves. The lack of speech rhythm that can result from blowing away your consonants is made good by the insertion of copious quantities of fucks and fucking, whose consonants are always given the full nine yards. In England there are many people whose speech is so dependent on the word fuck that they're virtually dumbstruck without it.

Typically in Estuary, all narratives are related in the present indicative:

> 'I sees Avril yesterday, and she says she's all set to go on her holidays, like, her bags is packed and all, and then the baby gets sick and she stays in-doors instead. So I says to her ...'.

Like it or not, Estuary English is here to stay, and can now be heard within a 100-mile radius of London. Anyone wishing to disguise a posh or regional accent can easily become adept at Estuary which is far easier to imitate than a genuine regional accent such as Scouse or Bristolian.

THE SPREAD OF ENGLISH

English is the nearest thing to a world language we've had since the days of the Roman Empire. At the end of the 18th century the majority of English speakers lived in England. Now it is the first language of around 400 million people and the second of perhaps 400 million more and is the official or semi-official language in more than 60 countries. It's the lingua franca of aviation, science, computing and business and is the common tongue of tennis players, golfers, racing drivers and others on the international sporting circuit. Three-quarters of the world's mail

HISTORY

is written in English. Whatever your mother tongue, if you want to make it in pop music, you sing in English. If you want to appear cool you salt your native tongue with words like cool and rock and super and mega, you call jeans jeans and trainers trainers and you say fuck a lot, the most internationally understood English word aside from OK and bar. And if you're gay, almost anywhere in the world now, you say you're gay, though you may not pronounce it like that.

NICK

To nick means to steal or to arrest, while the nick is a prison or police station.

So, if you nick something, you could be nicked and wind up in the nick.

But in the second half of this century, the rise of English has been an American affair. In the postwar era, the Marshall Plan and the permanent American garrisons from the Rhine to the Philippines ensured that the gospel of rock 'n' roll, Hollywood, Levi's and cheeseburger culture would be heard in every corner of the globe. After 1945, talking American meant talking money, and everyone wants to talk that. With it has come the language of marketing. Nowhere in the world does anything cost $5.00 any more, it's always $4.99. Flights to faraway places start from $499. Skimmed milk is 98% fat free, never 2% fat and orange-coloured liquid that hasn't been near an orange is pure orange drink with all natural ingredients. Natural is possibly the most abused word of the past 25 years.

America has also led the way with so-called politically correct English, starting with the feminist insistence on the maritally neutral title Ms. And why not, although it's curious that feminists in the *Fraulein/Frau, Mademoiselle/Madame, Signorina/Signora* cultures haven't campaigned for anything similar. In due course we've been exhorted to abandon 'disabled' for differently abled and 'deaf', 'dumb' and 'blind' for aurally, verbally and visually challenged. Time will tell whether these confections become part of the living language, although it's hard to see what purpose they serve other than to obscure the truth. Is blind a bad word? Is it pejorative? Does being visually challenged help you see any better? American English has developed a taste for euphemisms which are little better than lies, such as the CIA using terminate with extreme prejudice to mean 'assassinate' or corporate bosses offering workers career enhancement opportunities when what they're doing is giving them the sack. When assessing the merits of politically correct English, one should bear in mind that America is the country that adopted the words rooster and donkey because it couldn't cope with the implications of 'cock' and 'ass'.

America has begun passing laws to preserve the dominance of English, in spite of a vast Spanish-speaking population, and in the European Union even the French and Germans are succumbing to *force majeure* and having to accept that English is the nearest thing there is to a common European tongue. In parallel with a resurgent European nationalism and a growing insistence on the right to conduct one's affairs in Irish or Catalán or Sardu, English has become the second language of choice of the majority (83%) of European school students. In international scope, no other language comes near it and, in a shrinking and increasingly homogeneous world, English seems destined to be the glue that holds the whole thing together.

HISTORY

ABBREVIATIONS USED IN THIS BOOK

adj	adjective
f	feminine
inf	informal
n	noun
m	masculine
p	plural
pol	polite
RP	Received Pronunciation (see pages 30 and 187)
v	verb

Some syllables have been bolded to indicate stress.

British English

PRONUNCIATION

The reason there's so little relation between spelling and pronunciation is that the English will go to any lengths to make other people look inferior and stupid. There'd be no point in Leicester Square or Worcestershire if the English couldn't laugh at Americans failing to pronounce them correctly.

It also serves to reinforce snobbery, which is why posh names are spelled the way they are – Featherstonehaugh, Cholmondeley and St John are pronounced *Fanshaw*, *Chumly* and *Sinjin* respectively.

S. Burgen

A great many words are pronounced differently in Britain from how they're pronounced in other English-speaking countries. The difference may lie in where the stress falls, or in the long or short sound of a vowel, or in the sound of a consonant, or in a combination of these, often changing the sound of a word so much the listener may not recognise it.

borough	*burr-a*
café	*caff* or *café*
clerk	*clark*
controversy	*con-tro-ver-see*
contribute	*con-tri-bute* or *con-tri-bute*
cervical	'i' pronounced as the 'i' in 'wine' or as the 'i' in 'bit'
decade	*d'-cade*

fillet	*fill-et*
furore	*fyur-or-ee* – notice the spelling isn't 'furor'
glacier	'a' pronounced as the 'a' in 'crass' or as the 'ay' in 'bay'
mall	*mal*
medicine	*med-sin* – notice, only two syllables
migraine	'i' pronounced as the 'e' in 'me' or as the 'y' in 'fly'
pasta	*pas-ta* – the first syllable rhymes with 'mass'
plaid	pronounced as *played* or as *plad*
privacy	*pri-va-see* – 'i' pronounced as the 'i' in 'bit'

ANOTHER ROUTE

Route in Britain is pronounced like *root*, otherwise people will think you're asking for a crushing defeat.

schedule	*shed-u-al* – not 'sked-yu-al'. However, hang on to the *sk* sound if you're a schemer or schismatic.
sexual	*sex-u-al* or *sek-shu-al*
solder	*sol-der* – not 'sodder'
speciality	*spe-she-al-i-ty* – notice the five syllables
urinal	*yur-i-nal* – 'i' pronounced as the 'i' in 'wine'
vaginal	*vaj-i-nal* – 'i' pronounced as the 'i' in 'wine'
vitamin	*vit-a-min* – 'i' pronounced as the 'i' in 'fit'
yogurt	*yo-gurt* – 'o' pronounced as the 'o' in 'hot'
zebra	*ze-bra* to rhyme with 'Deborah' or as *zee-bra*
z	The letter 'z' is prounounced *zed*, not 'zee'

PLACENAMES

Britain is like any other country in that many of its placenames aren't pronounced as they are spelled. Foreigners – including English-speaking foreigners – are instantly spotted by pronouncing placenames exactly as they're spelled, whereas the natives know where the sounds are muffled, or shortened, or cut out altogether. It always jars on the Canadian's ear when the foreign speaker of English says Newfoundland, pronouncing it just like that, 'New-found-land' because Canadians say *New-f'nd-l'nd*. The same goes for Americans when they hear the state of Maryland pronounced 'Mar-ee-land' because they say *Mar-i-l'nd*. So it is for the British when foreign speakers of English massacre their placenames. However, there are a few general rules you can follow.

-erk

words and placenames containing the letters -erk are pronounced with an *ark* sound (clerk is pronounced *clark* and Clerkinwell as *Clark-in-well*)

-shire

the suffix -shire, meaning 'county', is pronounced *sher*, thus Buckinghamshire is *Buck-ing-h'm-sher*

-folk

the suffix -folk is clipped into the sound *f'k* with almost no vowel pronounced (Suffolk is pronounced *Suf-f'k*)

-mouth

the suffix -mouth is muffled into the sound *muth* or even *m'th* (Portsmouth is *Ports-m'th*)

-land

the suffix -land is clipped into the sound *l'nd* (Northumberland is *Nor-thum-ber-l'nd*)

PRONUNCIATION

-burgh

the suffixes -burgh and -borough are pronounced as *burra*, never as 'burg' or 'boro'. *Burra* is often run together like one syllable, thus Peterborough is ***Peet****-er-bra*.

-ham

when -ham is at the end of a word, it's simply cut to *um* (Durham is pronounced ***Dur****-um*)

internal y

when y is within a word, as in Derbyshire, it gets a quick short 'i' sound as in 'it', thus ***Dar****-bi-sher*

silent w

in most English placenames, the w in the suffix is silent, so Warwick is pronounced ***War****-ick*

Armed with these rules, you can figure out the pronunciation of many towns and counties as you go.

Berkeley Square	***Bark****-ley* Square
Berkshire	***Bark****-sher*
Cheltenham	***Chel****-ten-um*
Chiswick	***Chis****-ick*
Cumberland	***Cum****-ber-l'nd*
Dartmouth	***Dart****-m'th*
Marlborough	***Marl****-bra*
Norwich	***Nor****-ich*
Norfolk	***Nor****-f'k*

ELEPHANT & CASTLE

The anglicisation of foreign words has sometimes come up with curious results. The London district Elephant and Castle is thought to be named after Eleanor of Castile, Spanish wife of Edward I.

PRONUNCIATION

> The English like to keep you guessing where they're from, so someone from Manchester is variously a Mancunian or a Scally, a Liverpudlian or a Scouser is from Liverpool, a Brummie comes from Birmingham, a Geordie from Newcastle and a Taffy from Wales. As for a Salopian – you guessed it – that's someone from Shropshire.
>
> S. Burgen

Many other names and placenames in England simply have their own singular pronunciation. Some of the better known ones are:

Gloucestershire	collapsed to three syllables, *Glos-ter-sher*
Holburn	*Ho-ben* – 'o' pronounced as the 'o' in 'no'
Keighley	two syllables, *Keeth-ly*
Leicester	two syllables, *Les-ter*, like the man's name
Salisbury	two syllables, *Sals-bry*
Southwark	with a silent 'w'. The first syllable is pronounced *suth*, so *Suth-ark* is similar to 'Southern'.
Thames	pronounced *Tems* to rhyme with 'gems'
Worcestershire	collapsed to three syllables, *Wus-ter-sher*
St John	pronounced, strangely enough, as a single word, in two syllables, with the stress on the first syllable, *Sin-jin*

PRONUNCIATION

WORDS BORROWED FROM SCOTTISH GAELIC

English	Gaelic		
bard	bard	*baard*	'poet'
ben	beinn	*beh-een*	'hill'
bog	bog	*bohk*	'soft, wet'
brogue	bròg	*brock*	'shoe'
caber	cabar	*caper*	'pole'
claymore	claidheamh mòr	*clyaf mor*	'big sword'
dune	dùn	*doon*	'heap'
galore	gu leòr	*gu lyor*	'plenty'
loch	loch	*loch*	'loch'
Sassenach	Sasannach	*Sasunach*	'person from England or the Scottish lowlands'
sporran	sporan	*sporan*	'purse'
strath	strath	*strah*	'mountain valley'

> 'You really must come and see us soon' – read 'If you call us we'll pretend we're out'. With all due respect ... No offence intended ... Don't get me wrong but ... Far be it for me to say but ... Beware, all these disclaimers preface a commentary on your profound ignorance.
>
> S. Burgen

GREETINGS

Hello and goodbye in Britain vary depending on where you are and who you're talking to. In general, a simple 'hello' and 'good-bye' will be fine. But there are pet phrases and dialect words in different areas which you might want to get in on. For instance, in the northern areas of England, people say tara for goodbye (pronounced *ta-rah)* or ay up as a casual greeting (pronounced *ay-oop*). In London Cockney, it's common to greet a friend Eh, me old China, which roughly means 'Hey mate'. In some Midlands and Northern areas, people passing each other on the street say Are you all right?, or more likely just All right?, which instinctively makes you want to say 'yes', but of course you should just say 'Fine thanks'. While it isn't necessary to use these local phrases – 'Hi' is perfectly OK – you'll want to know what they mean when you hear them.

SAYING HELLO	
London	Watcha.
Liverpool	Ay up.
Newcastle	How?
Bristol	Oroit, me old lover?

MEETING PEOPLE

SOME TERMS OF ADDRESS

guv(ner)
> from 'governor', a respectful term of address for
> an owner or boss, but may be used with irony

love
> honey; sweetie; my dear. A common term
> of casual or friendly address in Britain.
> Shopkeepers and bus drivers might call you
> love when giving you your change or talking
> with you. It doesn't mean anything.

mate
> friend/buddy/pal. Also used in casual address,
> as in Pardon me mate, do you have the time?

The British may say they disdain the use of first names unless
they know each other, but this isn't true – people in Britain
use first names all the time with people they've just met. They
don't, however, extend their hand to a stranger with friendly
enthusiasm and say, 'Hi, I'm Ken'. It's a good rule in Britain, as
anywhere, not to use a person's first name unless you've been
invited to or if that's the way they've been introduced. If your
friendly hotel receptionist wears the name tag 'Jane Goode' and
you want to get her attention, call her 'Miss Goode', not 'Jane'.

As to please and thank you, the British are perhaps somewhat
overzealous on the please and never omit it. Elsewhere, an
attendant would sit at a table at a bazaar with a sign reading 'Pay
Here'. But in Britain, the sign would read 'Please Pay Here'. This
strict use of please can be off-putting to a foreigner while
shopping. Cashiers, after ringing up your items, will always state
the amount you owe followed by the word please, as though to
say 'May I have the money please'. Even if you already know how

much you owe and are extending it to them in your hand, they'll still look at you and say 'Two pounds ten please'. They aren't being rude or unobservant, just stating the amount, and the 'please' automatically comes with it.

Regarding the 'thank you', it's very common in Britain to say cheers as a casual version of 'thanks' (which can also mean 'goodbye'. In the Midlands of England and other parts, they say ta (pronounced *tah*).

PEOPLE & OCCUPATIONS

agony aunt
   writer of advice column for people with problem love-lives

barrister
   lawyer who argues cases in court. Unlike a solicitor, who prepares the client's case out of court and usually retains a barrister to argue it in court, a barrister actually pleads the case in court. A barrister has been 'called to the bar'.

caretaker
   janitor

charwoman/charlady
   cleaning woman/lady

collier
   coal miner

dustman
   trashman; garbage collector

farrier
   blacksmith

gaffer
   boss; foreman; school principal

newsagent
> person who runs a newspaper shop. Newsagents also sell items like sweets, soft drinks, magazines and stationery supplies. Many newsagents also have a small post office where customers can pay bills, buy stamps and send mail.

lollipop lady/man
> crossing guard at school crossings

pensioner
> senior citizen

sister
> head nurse on a hospital ward

solicitor
> lawyer who prepares a case for a client and usually retains a barrister to argue the case in court. A solicitor has not been 'called to the bar' as a barrister has.

train spotter
> someone who 'collects' train numbers by seeing how many different trains they can identify by number and then recording them. It's a deprecatory term in Britain which implies a person is dull. The term is familiar outside Britain now because of the movie.

twitcher
> birdwatcher

vicar
> clergyman in the Anglican Church or Church of England

CHILDREN

bairn	baby (Northern England and Scotland)
child minder	baby-sitter
cot	crib

MEETING PEOPLE

crèche	day nursery where parents can take their babies and pre-schoolers
cuddly toy	stuffed toy animal
dummy	pacifier
nappy	diaper
pram	buggy; baby carriage
push chair	stroller

TELEPHONE TALK

A few tips on telephone talk in Britain will help you avoid possible confusion.

blower

a slang term for the phone is the blower, which harks back to the old tube you had to blow into to get the attention of the person at the other end, then talked into. In some other countries, the equivalent is the 'horn'.

directory enquiries

when you need a phone number in Britain, you call directory enquiries, not 'information'. The number is 192 all over Britain. In England, the number for the operator is 100 and Emergency Services is 999 (fire, police, ambulance, coastguard, mountain rescue and cave rescue).

MEETING PEOPLE

The weather. It's always acceptable to open a conversation – even with a stranger – about the weather. The main thing is to complain that it's too hot or cold or wet or whatever. When confronted with an incontestably beautiful day, the correct phraseology is, 'Lovely day, isn't it? Can't last though'.

S. Burgen

engaged
>   when the line's already occupied, it's engaged, not 'busy'.
>   There's no such term as a 'busy signal', you simply say
>   'The line's engaged'.

ex-directory
>   unlisted. If you ring directory enquiries you might be told
>   the number you want is ex-directory, which means it's
>   unlisted.

'Is that ...'
>   the equivalent of 'Who's there?' (Is that Jenny?)

on the phone
>   if someone asks if you're on the phone, they want to know
>   if you have access to a private telephone

ring
>   the British ring people up, rather than 'call' them up
>   (What time did he ring?)

MEETING PEOPLE

SLANG & EXPRESSIONS

The British are notoriously foul-mouthed. In the 15th century Joan of Arc gave them the epithet *les goddams* – by the 1960s they'd been renamed *les fuckoffs*. Large numbers of British people drape their entire discourse around the word fuck, with the occasional wanker or bastard thrown in for colour. Those at the cutting edge are moving towards a sort of Zen English in which fuck will be the only word – shaped, nuanced and spat out to convey every thought and sentiment.

S. Burgen

SLANG

advert
  short for advertisement

argy-bargy
  (pronounced *ah-jy bah-jy*) argument; a bit of wrangling

bent
  not altogether legal; corrupt

the bill; old bill
  the police

blimey
  expression of surprise or contempt

bloody hell
  exclamation meaning anything from 'damn it' to something milder like 'wow'

SLANG & EXPRESSIONS

bloody

if someone calls you a **bloody idiot** they mean something like a 'big idiot' or 'stupid idiot'. Or they may say something like, 'He can just bloody well wait', which amounts to 'He can just damn well wait'.

bloody-minded

stubborn; persistent; obstinate; intentionally difficult

bleeding

now a euphemism for **bloody** but once considered genuine swearing

bloke

man

blotto

so tired as to be vacant headed; drunk

bobby

police officer. The term comes from Robert Peel, the British Prime Minister who established the Metropolitan Police Force in 1828 when he was Home Secretary. Its officers were called **bobbies** after Peel's first name, or **Peelers** after his second. They replaced the first police officers in England, who were called the 'Bow Street runners' because their beat was an area emanating outward from the magistrates' court in Bow Street.

botched/bodged job

poor quality repairs

bonk

have sex (Don't go in there, Arthur and Sharon are **bonking** .)

bottle

courage (He doesn't have the **bottle** to ask her.)

bugger
  scamp/scoundrel/pest (The little bugger.)

to bugger
  to break; to foul up; to spoil (Bloody hell, now all our plans are buggered.)

bugger off
  get lost

bugger all
  nothing; not a thing (He's got bugger all in the bank; I give bugger all what you think.)

chuffed
  delighted

daft
  crazy/stupid

dodgy
  (pronounced with an 'o' as in 'hot') questionable/awkward (I wouldn't buy that cheap watch, it looks dodgy.) The straight definition of this word is 'cunning' or 'artful', so Dickens' Artful Dodger would have been dodgy in the literal sense, but you'll most often hear it used in the colloquial sense.

the dole
  financial aid provided to the unemployed by the state – similar to welfare in other countries. Taking it is called being on the dole.

dosh
  (pronounced with an 'o' as in 'hot') money/cash

dotty
  feeble-minded/silly/absurd

fagged
  exhausted

fags
cigarettes

to fiddle
to cheat, especially on paying income tax

flog
sell

grass
inform on someone

kip
a nap or short sleep

knickers
women's underpants

the lads
the boys (meaning men as well as teenage boys). The lads
are the guys you typically go to the pub with. This word
often has a mischievous connotation, as in, 'I didn't do well
in school because I was too busy being a lad'.

knackered
tired; worn out

lolly
money

naff
tacky/unfashionable/daggy

nick
to steal/arrest

the nick
prison; police station

nooky
sexual activity

nutter
nut; crazy person

peckish
hungry for a snack

pissed
drunk

ponce
ostentatious or effeminate man. Also to borrow
(usually permanently).

potty
foolish/crazy

DID YOU KNOW ... Cheddar cheese only
became widely known when
people began visiting
Cheddar Gorge and taking
home the local cheese.
Cheddar was just one of
many Somerset villages
that produced this type of
cheese.

Over the years, Cheddar has
become a generic name
for any pale yellow,
medium-hard cheese.
The quality ranges from
supermarket Cheddar to
tangy and delicious farm-
house varieties.

SLANG & EXPRESSIONS

slippy
slippery/quick

to snog
to kiss

sod

derogatory term derived from 'sodomy'. Most British people who use this term don't mean anything sexually menacing by it, any more than meaning someone's dad isn't his real father when you call them a bastard. A person who calls you a **sod** just means to call you a stupid bastard or a jerk or something of the sort, so you may consider yourself insulted, but not too much.

sod off
get lost

sod it
damn it

stumm
to keep stumm means to keep quiet (from German *stumm* or Yiddish *shtum*, meaning 'mute')

ta
(pronounced *tah)* thanks

tara
(pronounced *tah-rah)* goodbye

telly
television

tosser
wanker/jerk

vet

to check something out. Can refer to anything from a scheme to be launched, to the quality of someone's work, to a candidate for a job. The word, strangely enough, derives from the verb 'vet' meaning to examine or treat an animal.

whinge
(rhymes with 'hinge') to whine or complain (Oh, stop whingeing). The word originated in Scotland but is now used in England as well.

willie
penis. (You've got to watch where your willie wanders.) Unlike other words you may know, this one is quite harmless and can be used in mixed company.

yob/yobbo
trouble-maker; hooligan; rowdy person

COMMON EXPRESSIONS

In most countries you'll find pet expressions. Here are a few terms and cliches you'll hear used regularly in Britain.

Albion
another name for Britain or England. The name may have been introduced into Britain by the Romans, who were struck – as we all are – by the White Cliffs of Dover when they landed in the 1st century (the Latin for 'white' is *albus).* The name could also be of Celtic origin (the Gaelic name for 'Scotland' being *Alba).*

at the bottom of the garden
this doesn't mean under the daisies where the bodies are buried. It just means at the furthest end of the back lawn or backyard.

at the end of the day
in the end; in the last analysis; ultimately

bits and bobs
odds and ends

not bothered
don't care (I'm not bothered whether or not we go.)

carrying the can
  left holding the responsibility

carry on
  continue what you're saying or doing (Turn left, then carry on down the road for another mile.)

chat up
  come on to; hit on

cock-up
  botched job; a screw-up. This colorful compound word can also act as a verb. (Look what you did, you cocked the whole thing up.)

come a cropper
  have a bad fall. Neck and crop means 'altogether', so the expression come a cropper means to fall to the ground completely. It's usually used metaphorically to mean that a plan or scheme has flopped.

SENT TO COVENTRY

During the Civil War (1644-49), Royalist troops imprisoned in St John's church in Coventry were ignored by the population, hence the expression sent to Coventry to describe someone who's being given the cold-shoulder. Some believe the expression arose when Royalist prisoners detained in Birmingham were moved to parliament-sympathising Coventry and suffered the same fate.

Lonely Planet

done
cheated/tricked (I was done out of my 20 quid.)

donkey's years
a very long time

a drop of
a glass of. If you go to a party or dinner in Britain and they ask if you'd like a drop of wine, don't expect to get just a drop – they'll bring you a normal glass of wine. So be careful – in Britain you can get bombed on five drops of wine.

early days
still early; too soon to know

effing and blinding
swearing excessively

fall out with
have a disagreement with; stop being friendly with

feel-good factor
sense of wellbeing. An emotional sort of barometer, this elusive factor is much discussed in British politics. It's used in other countries as well, but not as commonly as in Britain.

get your own back
get even with; get revenge

gone off
when referring to food, gone off means to have gone bad or spoiled. (The meat's gone off.) In general, it means to have lost interest in. (I've gone off the idea.)

gone missing
lost/disappeared (The cat's gone missing.)

grasp the nettle
>   take hold of the situation (sort of a cross between 'take the
>   bull by the horns' and 'bite the bullet')

had done with
>   was through with (I had done with him.)

hard done by
>   unfairly dealt with; having bad luck

in the event
>   in the end; in the final instance. In British English, this
>   phrase doesn't need to be followed by 'that' as in 'In the
>   event *that* this happens ...'. It can simply mean 'when the
>   outcome finally came'. (We were going to spend our holiday
>   in Greece, but in the event, we just stayed at home.)

in the first instance
>   in the first place

... isn't it; ... didn't he
>   quintessentially British expressions which are tacked on to
>   the end of a statement. In Britain, when people give an
>   opinion, they won't allow you to just be quiet and stay out
>   of trouble – you have to agree. Of course you can also flatly
>   disagree, which makes you feel like you're not cooperating.
>   What starts out as a plain statement always surprises you by
>   turning into an interrogative in the end, at which point
>   you're expected to participate – 'Sarah will never change, will
>   she?'. Won't she? Maybe you don't know, so you just smile
>   and nod. Even more disconcerting is the British habit of
>   asking you to corroborate things you couldn't possibly
>   know. 'I finally had a date with Sally last night, and I spilled
>   a drink all over her, didn't I?'. How should you know, you
>   weren't there. Sometimes it's a snappish retort to put the
>   other person on the wrong foot – 'John, you're here, we've

been waiting for over an hour'. The reply – 'Well I was stuck in traffic, wasn't I?'. Once you learn the game, it ceases to be intimidating. Just keep smiling, nodding, and looking non-committal.

it's throwing it down
it's pouring; it's raining cats and dogs

jam tomorrow
a common expression in Britain meaning if you do without things today (eat your toast plain), you'll be rewarded with bounty tomorrow (jam on your toast)

Drugs

If you were born after 1950 there's a very high probability that you use or have used illegal recreational drugs. Although there are constantly new vogue words, there seems now to be a Standard English for procuring these.

So, dope or black is hashish and grass or green is cannabis (relatively less available); skunk is super-strength marijuana; acid is LSD; coke or Charlie is cocaine; E or pills is ecstasy; smack, horse or H is heroin; speed or whizz is amphetamine; and Class A is any one of heroin, cocaine or amphetamine (in reference to their legal classification).

You no longer 'go out to score', you get sorted. And if you do, you'll need to know that the police are called the cops, filth, or the old Bill, and invariably the bizzies in Liverpool.

S. Burgen

look after
> take care of someone or something

meant to
> supposed to; should (It's a joke, Sue, you're meant to laugh.)

miss out
> omit (Kathy, you missed out three people on this invitation list.)

the odd ...
> the occasional ... When a British weather forecaster says, 'We may get the odd shower', she doesn't mean there are a lot of showers out there and the one that looks a bit strange may be coming our way.

not half ...
> very ... (He's not half funny, meaning he's hilarious.)

over the moon
> thrilled; blissfully happy

not on
> not right; it won't do (You're always late – it's just not on.)

be on about
> talk excessively about something (What's old Crabshanks on about this time?)

one-off
> one-time occurrence; fluke

over the top
> too much; overdoing it

over the way
> across the street

pack it in
> quit/finish. To quit your job in Britain is to pack it in. This expression's also used in phrases like, 'We've done enough work for today, Stephen. Let's pack it in'.

put pay to
    put an end to; finish off

right the way
    all the way; right through (Right the way down the country,
    the economy's improving.)

roger
    (of a man) to have sex with

Sloane Ranger
    wealthy, superficial, but well-connected young person. Taken
    from Sloane Square, an expensive London shopping and
    residential district, and the 'Lone Ranger'.

sort it out
    straighten it out; figure it out; fix it. Often this is
    shortened simply to sort it or may be phrased get it sorted.

sort someone out
    straighten someone out; give someone a piece of your mind

special offer
    on special; on sale. (Guinness is on special offer this week.)
    If you ask if Guinness is 'on sale', the shopkeeper might
    think you're simply asking if they have it for sale.

a spot of
    a little bit of; a portion of (a spot of tea/rain/trouble)

straight away
    immediately

table the topic
    put a topic on the agenda; discuss a topic. In Britain, tabling the
    topic does *not* mean shelving it or postponing it indefinitely.

take the Mickey/piss out of
    tease and humiliate – 'Relax, he's just taking the Mickey out of
    you' meaning 'Don't take offence, he's just making you look
    like a moron'. This expression is often abbreviated to simply

take the Mickey – 'Relax, he's just taking the Mickey'. To take the piss out of someone means the same thing.

takeaway (food)

take-out (Let's get a Chinese takeaway tonight.)

that ...

so ... Many British people use that where other English speakers would use 'so'. (It was that boring, half the audience went to sleep.)

there's no question

there's no possibility; it's out of the question. This is an important variant in usage, because it can cause misunderstanding. When the British say, 'There's no question of troops being sent in' they mean 'There's no chance of troops being sent in'. To other speakers of English, the same phrase could mean the opposite, 'There's no doubt of troops being sent in'.

the way forward

the best way to proceed; the right thing to do

work out

figure out (Let's work out the cost of a week in Spain compared to a week in France.)

BRAND NAMES

These brand names have either become synonymous with the generic product, or are in widespread use.

Baco Foil

aluminium foil

Docs

Doctor Martens boots

Domestos
  liquid bleach

Durex
  condom (the British slang for it is rubber johnny)

Harris tweed
  hand-woven tweed made in Harris, in the Outer Hebrides,
  and a very popular material for jackets and caps

Hoover
  vacuum cleaner. In Britain, vacuuming the house is
  hoovering it, no matter what brand of vacuum cleaner
  you're using. In current disputes over North Atlantic fishing
  rights, British fishermen worry that some other countries
  may hoover the seas clean.

Land Rover
  all-terrain vehicle

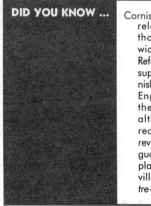

DID YOU KNOW ... Cornish, a Celtic language related to Welsh, is thought to have been widely spoken until the Reformation, when it was suppressed after a Cornish uprising against the English. It died out in the 19th century, and although efforts have recently been made to revive it, the Cornish language mainly lives on in place names of Cornish villages that begin with tre-, meaning 'settlement'.

Levi's or Wranglers
   jeans

Nescafé
   instant coffee

Schweppes
   tonic water; drinks mixer

TCP
   antiseptic ointment

Tipp-ex
   whiteout

WD-40
   automotive lubricant in a spray can

Wedgwood
   fine china

Weetabix
   popular breakfast cereal

Zimmer frame
   walking aid; walker

SLANG & EXPRESSIONS

Cockney is probably best known for its rhyming slang. Words appearing in brackets give the full form that the rhyme depends on, but often just the first part is used, as in

He slipped and fell on his Khyber.

Can I give you a goose's for that?

The spellings taters and scarper reflect Cockney pronunciation, and can be found in dictionaries in their own right.

Abergavenny	penny
airs and graces	races/faces/braces
Anna Maria	fire
apples and pears	stairs
April Fool	stool/tool
Aristotle	bottle
Army and Navy	gravy
Artful Dodger	lodger
Auntie Ella	umbrella
babbling brook	crook
bacons (and eggs)	legs
ball of chalk	walk
Barnaby Rudge	judge
Barnet (Fair)	hair
bat and wicket	ticket
Bath bun	sun
bees and honey	money
beggar my neighbour	labour

COCKNEY

boat race/Chevy Chase	face
Bo Peep	sleep
bow and arrow	sparrow
bread and butter	gutter
bread and cheese	sneeze
Brussels (sprouts)	scouts
bubble and squeak	beak (magistrate)
bucket and pail	jail
burnt cinder	window
Burton (on Trent)	rent
bushel and peck	neck
butcher's (hook)	to look Let's have a butcher's.
Cain and Abel	table
Cape of Good Hope	soap
Captain Cook	book
cash and carried	married
cat and mouse	house
china (plate)	mate
cobblers (awls)	balls
cock linnet	minute
cock-sparrow	barrow
country cousin	dozen
currant (bun)	son
Daily Mail	tale
daisy roots	boots
dickory dock	clock
dicky bird	word
dig in the grave	shave

dog and bone	phone
dustbin lid	kid
elephant's trunk	drunk
field of wheat	street
fife and drum	bum
fisherman's (daughter)	water
frog (and toad)	road
gay and frisky	whisky
ginger beer	queer/engineer
Glasgow Ranger	stranger
goose's (neck)	cheque
Harry Randall	candle
holy friar	liar
Isle of Wight	right
Jack and Jill	till/hill
Jack (Jones)	alone
Jack the Ripper	kipper (smoked herring)
Jimmy Riddle	piddle (pee)
Joanna	piano
Khyber (Pass)	arse
Lillian Gish	fish
loaf (of bread)	head
merchant banker	wanker
mince pies	eyes
monkey's tail	nail
Mother Hubbard	cupboard
Mutt and Jeff	deaf
north and south	mouth

COCKNEY

Oliver (Twist)	fist
on the floor	poor
Oxford (scholar)	dollar
peas (in the pot)	hot
pen (and ink)	stink
	That cheese pens a bit.
pimple and blotch	scotch
plates of meat	feet
pleasure and pain	rain
pony and trap	crap
porkies (pork pies)	lies
	Have you been telling porkies again?
taters 'potatoes (in the mould)'	cold
rabbit (and pork)	to talk
	He was rabbiting on for hours.
raspberry ripples	nipples
read and write	fight
Richard the Third	bird/turd
round the houses	trousers
rub-a (-dub-dub)	pub
salmon and trout	stout
scarper 'Scapa (Flow)'	go
Sexton (Blake)	cake
skin and blister	sister
stand at ease	cheese
tiddly (wink)	drink

tin flute	suit
thrups (thrupenny bits)	shits/tits
titfer (tit for tat)	hat
Tom and Dick	sick
Tom Thumb	rum
weeping willow	pillow
weasel and stoat	coat

So a Cockney might – at least in theory – be heard to say:

'I don't bleedin' Adam and Eve it – I went out to get some Uncle Fred, a Linen Draper, and some Oily Rags, and when I reached for my Sausage and Mash I found the Tea Pot Lid had fallen out of my Lucy Locket/Sky Rocket. So now I'm totally Hearts of Oak!'

If you can't make head or tail of this, here's a couple of clues: oily rags are fags – cigarettes, remember! – and a tea pot lid is a quid, or £1. Political correctness hasn't had much effect on the use of rhyming slang – the term trouble and strife for wife is still used, while a woman's Bristols are her breasts (Bristol City is a football team, thus Bristol Cities = titties). Occasionally the link between a slang term and the word it rhymes with is difficult to work out – if you hear the term He's lost his bottle (He's lost his nerve), you have to know that the origin of bottle is 'bottle of beer' ('fear' – so what's literally 'He's lost his fear' in fact means just the opposite). And new rhyming slang comes in and out of fashion all the time – more recent forms are Hank (or Lee) Marvin for 'starving', or Gregory Pecks for 'specs' (spectacles). And so on. But don't be dismayed – the average Londoner doesn't actually use very much rhyming slang, if any, in day-to-day conversation, and most of the time you can work out from the context what is meant.

The pronunciation of Cockney may be more of a problem, though. Listen out for the heavy use of glottal stops (a catch in the throat, as when coughing) in butter, Battersea or lottery and the dropping of h at the beginning of words like Harry, Hampstead or Harvey Nichols (the famous department store, or rhyming slang for pickles). The letter l can often sound like *w*, as in *miwk* 'milk', while the use of 'f' and 'v' for the th sounds in thought and mother ends up making these words sound like *fought* and *muvva*. More and more Londoners are starting to use an r sound that sounds more like a 'w' as well, so that three, for example, can often sound like *fwee*. The vowels of Cockney are similar to those of broad Australian accents, which is one reason why Londoners and Australians often get mistaken for one another.

GETTING AROUND

TRAINS

Train travel in Britain is notoriously unreliable. If you're stranded for hours because your train ran out of fuel 50 metres from the station, you might be told your train's been delayed due to it running late.

A recent survey found Britain's rail system to be less efficient than those of India, China and Pakistan, and even with high-tech intercity rolling stock, British Rail is less punctual than Ghana's national railway, which uses steam engines built 40 years ago! Britain also has Europe's most expensive railway – pricier even than Switzerland's.

Because it's overloaded and unable to cope, the train and underground companies have for many years followed the eminently sensible policy of pricing their potential customers back into their cars. However, it is possible to buy reasonably priced tickets, by agreeing to travel at the time most inconvenient to you. For example, if you want to get from London to Manchester for a lunchtime meeting and back the same day, you can do it, but the ticket will cost about the same as a return to Bangkok. However, if you're prepared to arrive at 8.15 pm and then hop back on a train to London 40 minutes later, the fare will be a complete bargain.

Bear this in mind when you see ads offering tickets from London to Edinburgh for little more than the price of a box of matches. The fare does exist, of course, (now why would they lie?) but to get it at that price you had to book at least six weeks before you were born, travel on a Tuesday between four and five in the morning and prove that you're a full time agronomy student. Oh, and they can't guarantee a seat and tickets are non-refundable.

D. Watt & S. Burgen

channel tunnel
> tunnel linking Britain with France through which high-speed passenger and vehicle rail services are run. Also known as the chunnel.

railway
> railroad

rolling stock
> train cars

subway
> an underground pedestrian passage. This isn't a place where trains run, like in New York. It's a way to get across a busy street by going under it rather than trying to cross through traffic.

the tube
    London's underground passenger railway service. Also
    known as the Underground.

way out
    exit

TAXI

Although the traditional black cab (which now comes in a
variety of colours) may not be the cheapest way to get around
London unless you're travelling in a group, you can be sure you'll
get where you want to go by the quickest possible route. In
order to get a licence, London's cabbies must memorise thousands
of streets within a six mile radius of Charing Cross, as well as the
position of clubs, hotels, theatres, railway stations and a host of
other locations.

Minicabs are freelance taxis that can only be hired by phone,
and are generally cheaper than black cabs.

CROSSING THE CHANNEL

On a clear day you can see across the English Channel
to France. You can make your way to the Continent by
plane, rail, ferry, catamaran, hovercraft, or, if you can
match the record, you could swim in less than eight hours.

BUSES

Buses run absolutely everywhere in and around cities with great
frequency, though service is thin to non-existent in villages and
hamlets. Buses have lately been privatised, and the competition
among different bus lines makes getting information a little less
than simple. But all in all, buses are efficiently run and the prices
are fair enough. In some cities, you have to have the right change
when paying your fare.

bus
> local bus (see also coach)

bus shelter
> bus stop

coach
> long-distance bus (see also bus)

FORMING A 'QUEUE'

A queue is a line or row of people. The word queue can also be used as a verb ('I had to queue for two hours'). In Britain, people queue, or stand in line, for buses and taxis. Sometimes the queue is loosely formed, and you won't even recognise it as a line – but the people standing there are perfectly aware of who's where in the haphazard queue. And in Britain, they don't skip ahead or jump the queue.

CAR

In England, the network of high speed roads that gets you from city to city is called the Motorway. Different sections of the motorway are identified by numbers, such as the M1 (going into London) or the M5 (going into Birmingham). These roads are well marked and easy to find your way around on. The speed limit on the Motorway is 70mph (112kph), though people tend to go faster. There aren't many speed limit signs on the Motorway– the national speed limit is simply learned before the driving test is taken. The speed limit in built-up areas is 30mph (48kph), and 40mph (64kph) in sparsely built-up areas. In outlying areas it's 60mph (96kph).

Roads aren't always well or consistently marked, either with speed limit signs or signs naming the road, which can be a problem for people trying to find their way around with a map.

Signs tend to be sparse or hard to see – for instance they don't occur at every corner or junction and you often have to drive annoying distances before you see a sign identifying the name of the street or road you're on.

When they do occur, they don't appear high on a pole at the corner or junction. Rather, they're placed on the sides of buildings, on walls that run alongside the roads, and in the dividing strip on dual carriageways on short posts a foot or two high. If a vehicle in the other lane is in the way, you miss the sign.

Finally, don't try to drive around Britain without a copy of the Highway Code, which can be purchased in any post office.

articulated lorry
    semi (large truck with cab and trailer attached by a joint or
    hitch)

bonnet
    hood

boot
    trunk

caravan
    camper/house trailer. In Britain a caravan has nothing
    to do with camels or a string of vehicles, it just means a
    live-in vehicle.

car park
    parking lot

circus
    open space or intersection in town, with streets converging
    on it (such as Piccadilly Circus in London and Colmore
    Circus in Birmingham)

diverted traffic
    detour

driving licence
> driver's licence

dual carriageway
> boulevard (broad road with dividing strip between the left
> and right sides of the road)

filter
> the green arrow on a stoplight indicating that cars in a
> turning lane may turn. Your passenger may say, 'You can go,
> you have a filter'.

gear stick
> gear shift

high beam
> brights

indicators
> blinkers

lay-by
> rest stop, but with no facilities

lorry
> truck

motorcar
> car

motorway
> freeway; autobahn; interstate highway

to overtake
> to pass another vehicle

mudguard
> fender. The word fender is used in Britain for the protective
> guard that goes in front of a fireplace. The metal piece
> of a car that goes over the tyre area is referred to as the
> mudguard, wheel arch or wing.

pelican crossing
 road crossing with pedestrian-activated traffic lights. Adapted
 from **pe**destrian **li**ght **con**trolled crossing.

petrol
 gasoline

roundabout
 intersection where traffic moves in a circular clockwise
 direction around a median point. For those who haven't
 encountered this, it's literally a 'round' set-up.

service area
 roadside/rest stop. Place where you can turn off the motorway to use the toilet, put petrol in your car or get something
 to eat.

tyre
 not only a Phoenician port in the Old Testament, but also,
 in Britain, the rubber wheel of a car

verge (of a road)
 shoulder (of a road)

windscreen
 windshield

windscreen wipers
 windshield wipers

zebra crossing
 pedestrian road crossing. Pedestrian crossings in Britain have
 black and white stripes painted on them, hence the name
 zebra crossing.

GETTING AROUND

BICYCLE

Renting a bicycle (and there are rental shops in many towns) is always a good idea when sightseeing, as things don't whizz past you on a bike as they do in a car, and it's a lot easier to park your bicycle than your car when you want to stop and look at something. But England could do a lot better with bicycle paths, and they intend to – plans are in the works for new bicycle paths across the country.

push bike
bicycle/two-wheeler (A bike in Britain commonly means a motorcycle.)

stabilisers
training wheels for a child's bicycle

ACCOMMODATION

The dream of any British person is to own their own home and Britain has a very high rate of home-ownership. The worst place to live is in a council (publicly owned) flat on an estate, while the height of aspiration is to own a detached (free-standing) house. Next best is semi-detached (two houses in one building) or if you must, a terrace, or row house. Failing that a flat. Below that is a bedsit, a one-room flat. A studio flat is merely a bedsit that you can't afford. A loft is an expensive flat carved out of some Victorian warehouse left over from Britain's glorious industrial past.

Hotels are much like any others in the developed world, apart from those housed in historic buildings. But the Bed and Breakfast (B&B), the equivalent of the European *pension*, is a truly British institution. A B&B is a cheap hotel and most are friendly, good value and serve the sort of breakfast that will save you from having to eat for the rest of the day. The majority of B&Bs are people's homes, and the owners usually live in some corner of the house that isn't let out. Running a B&B is a traditional way of making some money on the side or of surviving redundancy in areas of high unemployment. So the management haven't necessarily started their B&B because they feel they have some vocation as hoteliers, and sometimes as a result guests get the feeling that they're an unwelcome but necessary evil intruding on the owners' privacy. This is quite likely the case. Most B&Bs are great, but if you feel unwanted it's because you *are* unwanted.

S. Burgen

HOUSING

bedsit

> bedsitting room is the full term for this rental
> accommodation, consisting of a combination bedroom
> and sitting room, similar to a studio flat

council house

> a house built by a local authority (town council) and leased,
> often at a subsidised rent

detached house

> free-standing house (not meaning that the house was once
> attached to some other building and has since been detached.
> It simply means a free-standing house, which always was so.)

digs

> lodgings; dwelling; place to stay

estate

> housing development, residential or industrial district
> planned by a town council or a private developer. People in
> Britain frequently speak of living on this estate or that estate.
> It rarely means the land and property held by one person or
> family. Most of the time it means a housing development.

flat

> apartment

inn

> pub with accommodation

terraced houses

> row houses. This is quite simply a row of houses, usually all
> built to the same plan and adjoining one another.

maisonette

> flat which is part of a house that's been subdivided. Each
> maisonette has a separate entrance, and usually has two, and
> sometimes three floors.

ACCOMMODATION

semi-detached house
  two houses joined by a common wal; a side-by-side

AROUND THE HOUSE

bath
  bathtub. The British say, He's in the bath rather than, 'He's
  in the tub'.

bin
  short for dustbin. The British often use bin as a verb as well
  ('Bin it', meaning 'Throw it in the bin').

curtain rails
  curtain rods

double glazing
  windows consisting of a double layer of glass to insulate
  against cold and damp. Neither pane is removable. In
  Britain, the storm windows and screens common in some
  other countries are virtually unknown. Most older homes
  don't have double glazing, and it's rather expensive to
  have installed.

dustbin
  wastebasket; garbage/trash can. The literal-minded person
  might think this is a container in which British people put
  their dust, but it isn't.

duvet
  (pronounced *doo-vay*) comforter/quilt/doona

en suite
  with bathroom included. If you stay at a hotel or B&B and
  your room is en suite, it means you have a toilet and a bath
  or shower with your room, not down the hall.

garden
  front or back yard. In Britain, the term garden doesn't just
  mean the area where flowers or vegetables are planted. It's

also the lawn or the yard. A yard can be an area that's used to store equipment or for vehicle access to a factory or warehouse. It's also a working area, as in the term stockyard or dockyard.

immersion heater
common term for a domestic hot water heater

lodger
renter/tenant/roomer

lounge
living room

wardrobe
moveable clothes closet. Most British homes don't have built-in bedroom closets but free-standing wardrobes.

wheelie bin
outdoor garbage bin on wheels

England can appear a very proscriptive society. No country puts up more signs, and nowhere more so than in the city. On public transport alone you'll encounter: Stand on the Left; Do Not Speak to the Driver; Please Have Exact Change; Mind the Gap; No Standing on Upper Deck; Pushchairs Must be Folded; You Must Have a Valid Ticket to Travel; Do Not Alight While Bus is in Motion.

Beside one of the outdoor bathing ponds on London's Hampstead Heath there's a sign which reads: 'Do Not Enter The Water From the Banks'. This is a masterpiece. A lesser authority would simply put up a sign saying 'No Swimming', but the Hampstead sign presents the law-abiding English person with a real challenge – how to get in.

The English also delight in overly polite signs such as Kindly Refrain From Smoking or The Management Respectfully Requests That Guests Do Not Take Visitors To Their Rooms. Or when you go to stay in a hotel and discover the place is in the throes of full-scale renovation, there is sure to be a sign that says, The Management Would Like To Apologise For Any Inconvenience Caused, which suggests that they'd like to but are damned if they will.

S. Burgen

borough

> urban community incorporated by a royal charter. A borough tends to be smaller than a city, and can be located within a city, as in the case of Greater London, which has 32 boroughs. Another difference between a borough and a city

is that a city has a cathedral. The Borough, which is the setting for a number of scenes in Charles Dickens' novels, is a specific small borough on the south-eastern stretch of the Thames. In early times, a borough tended to be fortified (walled-in) – the Old English word 'burg' meant a fortified town. The spelling for this, in Middle English, advanced to 'burgh' which can be seen as part of the formation of today's word borough

canteen
> snack bar; refreshment room (found in places like universities, schools and hospitals)

the City
> the 'square mile' of Inner London on the north bank of the Thames. When people talk about the City, they're talking about the part of London which is governed by the Lord Mayor and the Corporation, and normally it refers especially to the commercial circles and business part of this area. The City also has several thousand residents.

city centre
> downtown/central business district. Despite the fact that for nearly two years half the country was singing *Downtown* along with Petula Clark, British people don't seem to know what it means. If you get on the bus and ask the driver, 'Are you going downtown?' you'll get a blank look. One American visitor recently called directory inquiries (information) to get the street address of the main downtown post office of the city he was in. The operator kept asking him where it was (not the post office but 'downtown'). The visitor, not being aware of the term city centre, tried numerous ways to make himself understood but when the operator finally said, 'Is it near Bromsgrove?' he gave it up for a lost cause.

Downing Street
> small street between Westminster Palace to the south (otherwise known as the Houses of Parliament) and the street called Whitehall to the north. It lets onto Parliament Street on the

east. All this is just as the Thames begins to arc eastward.
Number 10 Downing Street is the residence of the Prime
Minister, and Number 11 is the residence of the Chancellor
of the Exchequer, so Downing Street and Number 10 are
terms often used synonymously with 'the Government'.

close
an enclosure or enclosed place, such as a street closed at one
end, a precinct of a cathedral, or a public school playing
field. Pronounced like *close* when it means 'near' rather than
'to shut', the word dates back to Medieval England and
originates from Old French *clos*.

common
an area of land, which is usually grassy, held in common
by all members of a community. The village green is
a common.

East End
working-class area within walking distance of the City, which
has a mix of Cockney, Indian, Bangladeshi and Jewish cultures.
Its attractions include offbeat museums and Indian cuisine.

FLEET STREET

Since the time of Caxton, people have had ink on their
fingers in this central part of London. Rupert Murdoch
changed all that in the mid-80s when he introduced
state-of-the-art, non-union printing presses at Wapping
in the Docklands redevelopment. The move from Fleet
Street was a tumultuous scrum of politicking and picket
lines, but it worked. Now all that remains are ghosts,
such as El Vino's, the journos' number one watering hole
and main source of inspiration, and the former *Daily
Express* building, an Art Deco structure of chrome, glass
and nautical curves that was always more dashing than
the newspaper itself.

D. Watt

first-class/second-class mail
two levels of mail delivery service – first class is marginally more expensive and is delivered faster

Fleet Street
street in London formerly devoted largely to the production and publication of daily newspapers

Harley Street
street in north-west London, celebrated for its high residency of doctors and specialists (called consultants)

high street
main street. An English high street is more, however, than just an equivalent to what is called a 'main street' elsewhere. Firstly, a high street is where the bulk of the shops are, it's not just the primary shady thoroughfare in town. On the high street, you'll find the butcher, the baker, the green-grocer, the newsagent, the chemist and perhaps a fish and chip shop. On many high streets people also pay their bills, visit the post office, and do their banking.

Secondly, the high street is an English tradition and, for many, an object of some affection. The English think of their high streets the way they do their hedgerows – as something intrinsically English. And like the hedgerows, the high streets are a part of the national heritage the English would like to see protected.

There's a movement in the country today to see a brake put on the building of huge shopping malls, which are springing up on city outskirts at a rapid rate. Many English people fear these malls could in time obliterate the traditional high streets and turn them into slums.

Leicester Square
popular place in London to hang out. Check out some of the antiquarian book shops in the district while you're there.

lock
part of a canal or river that can be closed off and the water levels changed to raise or lower boats

Lombard Street

    street in London containing many of the principal London banks. The term is used to refer to the setting of high finance and the stock market in Britain. Literature enthusiasts may recall that, in Thackeray's *Vanity Fair*, the ruined Sedley and the prosperous Osborne did business in Lombard Street.

London

    capital of England and of the United Kingdom. London is the seat of the Crown and home of the British Parliament, with the Thames River flowing west to east more or less through the middle of the city. What many tourists regard as London, however, is actually two cities and their environs – London to the east and Westminster to the west. The dividing point is Temple Bar and the Inns of Court. Greater London's population comprises almost a quarter of the total population of England.

    The ancient City of London, now known as the City, is roughly a square mile area once enclosed within the old medieval city walls, with their seven gates – Ludgate, Newgate, Aldersgate, Cripplegate, Moorgate, Bishopsgate and Aldgate. It's bounded by the Aldgate Underground and the Tower of London on the east, the Thames on the south, Temple Bar and the Inns of Court on the west, and, approximately, London Wall Street on the north.

    Traditionally, when the monarch enters the city of London in state (she, of course, lives in Westminster, in Buckingham Palace), the Lord Mayor of London greets him or her and offers his sword, which the monarch immediately returns. This squares things for entry into the City. In former times, the gate or bar, depending upon where the sovereign entered (today it's normally Temple Bar), was not raised until this ritual was performed.

the Met

    the London Metropolitan Police Department. Also, the official London Weather Office.

mews
> dwellings or lodgings grouped around an open yard or alley.
> The word mews has a developing history. In medieval times,
> it referred to a set of cages for keeping hawks during moult-
> ing. Later, it designated the royal stables at Charing Cross in
> London, built on the site of the royal hawk mews. Later
> still, it meant any set of stables grouped around an open yard
> or alley. Eventually, mews were converted into lodgings, and
> in the 19th century, rows of town houses were actually built
> in the style of mews. Mews is today a designation for an
> address, and you'll find it on street maps just like streets
> or lanes, for example Glynde Mews or Halkin Mews
> in London.

minster
> cathedral

Naffy
> N.A.A.F.I. (Navy, Army and Air Force Institutes.) Naffy is
> the nickname for a canteen catering to members of the
> armed services. It sells provisions and alcohol, and usually
> includes a bar and lunch-counter in a camp or barracks.

Old Lady of Threadneedle Street
> Bank of England. Located on the east side of London on –
> you guessed it – Threadneedle Street.

pavement
> sidewalk; paved pedestrian walkway

post/pillar box
> mail box

Scotland Yard
> London's famous crime detection agency, sometimes just called
> The Yard. It moved from just off Whitehall in 1891 – when
> the fictional Sherlock Holmes was practicing criminal detection
> – to Parliament Street. At that point it changed from 'Great
> Scotland Yard' to 'New Scotland Yard'. In 1967, it moved to
> where Broadway meets Victoria Street, midway between
> Westminster Cathedral and Westminster Abbey.

South Bank

enclave of arts venues, roughly situated between Hungerford
Railway Bridge and Waterloo Bridge, on what's traditionally
known as the wrong side of the river

vault

in many English-speaking countries, a vault is where money
is kept in a bank. But in Britain, vaults are also burial places
for people of rank or wealth. They're found in churches and
cathedrals, beneath the marble floor or above it in
encasements, often magnificently carved, often with effigies
of the person buried within lying prone on the vault. They
exist, of course, in church graveyards as well.

Some of the more famous people you'll meet will be
long in their graves, like the host of kings and queens buried
in Westminster Abbey, along with the illustrious authors
encrypted beneath the floor in Poets' Corner, and famous
figures like bad old King John in a Cathedral in Worcester.

venue

location; site; meeting place

West End

theatre district in Westminster where world-class drama and
comedy are performed. Similar to New York's Broadway.

Westminster

a city to the west of and adjoining London. Westminster is a
city in itself, even though the term Westminster is also used to
refer to Parliament. The Palace of Westminster and the Houses
of Parliament are one and the same. It was one of Henry VIII's
royal residences until it was damaged by fire in 1512.
Westminster Hall is the oldest surviving part of the palace.

Some of the landmarks of London are actually in the city
of Westminster, not the city of London. Among these are
Westminster Abbey, Westminster Cathedral, Buckingham
Palace, St James's Palace, Pall Mall, Trafalgar Square, the
National Gallery, Charing Cross, Leicester Square, the West
End theatre district, Covent Garden, Victoria Station,

Harrod's department store, Hyde Park, Kensington Palace and Gardens, Piccadilly Circus, Soho, the British Museum, Bloomsbury, 122B Baker Street (ostensible home of Sherlock Holmes and Doctor Watson), and Scotland Yard.

Westminster Abbey

ancient cathedral in Westminster. Most English monarchs since William I have been crowned in Westminster Abbey, and until 1760, most were also buried there. It's situated between the Houses of Parliament and Westminster School.

Whitehall

the term Whitehall can be confusing to visitors. Is it a royal palace? Is it a street? Is it a group of government offices? The answer is yes to all three.

It's a street where major government offices are located. Both the street and the offices take their name from the Palace of Whitehall, used from the time of Henry VIII to William III.

Whitehall once stretched from the Cross in the village of Charing to St James's Park, which borders another royal residence, St James's Palace. It boasted landscaped terraces and gardens, aviaries, opulent staterooms, a waterside gallery which extended out over the Thames, a tennis court, a tiltyard for jousters, a bowling green, and a cockpit.

The Palace was destroyed by fire in 1698, except for the Banqueting House, which still stands between Richmond Terrace and Horseguards Avenue, with Victoria Embankment on the east and Parliament Street on the west.

IN THE COUNTRY

Most countries have both naturally occurring and constructed topographical features with which they're identified, like Australia's outback, Russia's steppes, Brazil's Amazon jungles, the US's everglades and bayous, and Holland's dikes and canals. Britain also has its special features, and their names may be unfamiliar to you.

barrow

prehistoric grave or burial mound. Numerous barrows exist in Britain and have been studied by archaeologists. If you've read Thomas Hardy's *The Return of the Native*, you'll remember Rainbarrow, which figures prominently in the novel. It protrudes on the rise of a section of heathland near Hardy's childhood home in Dorset.

bridleway

path that can be used by walkers, horse riders and cyclists

the Broads

a low-lying area of wetlands in the county of Norfolk, more specifically called the Norfolk Broads

downlands/downs

treeless, undulating chalk uplands of south and southeast England and elsewhere, traditionally a major source of pasturage (no, you didn't misread – the downlands are uplands). You may have heard of the famous racecourse Epsom Downs, which is located on the downs of Surrey.

earthwork

an embankment or fortification made of earth. Numerous earthworks exist in England – some of them built by the Romans, some by earlier inhabitants – which have been the subject of archeological studies. One such prehistoric earthwork is just north of the seaside resort town of Weymouth, on the Channel. It's called Maiden Castle, and serves as the subject of one of Thomas Hardy's short stories, *A Tryst at an Ancient Earthwork*. He makes it come to life with an eeriness and forboding so powerful that one critic has said the earthwork itself is the main character in the story.

fen
low, marshy or flooded tract of land

firth
a river estuary, such as the Firth of Forth and the Firth of Clyde in Scotland. It's related to the Norse word *fjord*.

footpath
path for walkers or hikers. In England, footpaths exist all over the country, including hundreds of ancient footpaths running through private lands which, by law, the owners aren't allowed to obstruct, plant over or destroy. Every British subject (and tourist) has the right to walk unimpeded on these footpaths, although the pedestrian must adhere to the path and not wander off onto the owner's land. They're usually marked with a sign reading 'Public Footpath' or, sometimes, 'Public Right of Way'.

furze
plant with sharp thick spines and small yellow flowers that grows on heathland and on other sandy patches. Also known as gorse in the north.

heath
tract of open wasteland, generally covered with low, patchy shrubs such as heathbells, milkwort, broom or furze

hedgerow
row of bushes forming a hedge. English hedgerows are notable for their size and for the wildlife they shelter. Either low or high hedges – often dotted with bright yellow

flowers of furze or gorse plants growing amid them – stretch unbroken for miles along the winding roads of England and between farmers' fields. Besides creating borders and giving a picturesque aspect to the landscape, they support a wide variety of animal life, including birds, small animals and insects. Thus, hedgerows are important to the ecology of England and are generally protected.

market town
market towns had their origins in the medieval period, when towns and cities began to spring up all over Europe. A town depended on trade to prosper and grow, but had to gain permission from the monarch, in the form of a royal charter, to hold regular markets. Towns which obtained such permission were designated market towns.

LETTERBOXING

If you're out walking in Dartmoor, you might stumble across one of the 4000 'boxes' that have been hidden throughout the countryside. Around 10,000 letterboxers take part in this massive treasurehunt, coming from as far as America, France and Belgium. The object is to find as many boxes as you can, sign the accompanying visitors' books and use the stamp provided to stamp your record book. There are even 'mobile boxes' – odd characters who wander around the moors waiting for a fellow letterboxer to approach them with the words 'Are you a travelling stamp?'. Once you've collected 100 stamps, you can apply to join the '100 Club', whose members receive a clue book with map references for other boxes.

Lonely Planet

moor

tract of open wasteland, generally covered with heather and devoid of trees. Emily Brontë's *Wuthering Heights* is set in the West Yorkshire moors.

mead

meadow

plantation

an area planted with trees. Many people associate the word 'plantation' with the tea plantations of India, the coffee plantations of Brazil, or the cotton plantations of the Old South in the US. A plantation in Britain is none of these, but an area of trees, mainly fir trees, purposefully planted for practical use.

wold

piece of open, uncultivated land, especially elevated country, moorland, or downland. The better known examples are the hilly districts of Leicestershire and Lincolnshire, the Yorkshire Wolds, or the Cotswolds in the West Country. The word probably derives from Old English, either from *wald* (Anglian for 'forest'), or from *weald* (West Saxon for 'a wooded district') – although these days wolds are largely treeless.

> You can't make jokes about awful English food any
> more. The days when even spaghetti was dismissed
> as foreign muck are past. The English have
> discovered cooking, and London is now one of the
> best cities in the world to eat in, although rural and
> small-town England is still reliably awful. In London,
> chip shops are practically extinct – going for a Ruby
> Murray (curry) is the gastronomic pastime.
>
> S. Burgen

FOOD

aubergine
  (pronounced *oh-ber-zheen* with a soft 'g' like the 's' in
  'pleasure') eggplant

bangers and mash
  sausages and mashed potatoes

bap
  bun/roll. Like a hamburger bun, but very wide and large.

beef roll
  ground beef and ham cooked in a pudding mould

beetroot
  beets

bill
  payment at a restaurant. You can ask for the bill, but not
  the 'check'. In Britain, a cheque is the thing you tear out
  of your chequebook.

FOOD & DRINK

biscuits
  cookies/crackers

blue Stilton
  world-class blue-veined cheese made in Leicestershire,
  Nottinghamshire and Derbyshire. Great with port wine.

caff
  café

caster sugar
  a finer sugar than regular sugar, and more expensive. Regular
  sugar in Britain is a bit coarser than in some other countries,
  and you might find caster sugar closer to what you're used to.

chips
  french fries

clotted cream
  cream so heavy or rich that it's become clotted or clumpy
  (but not sour)

corn
  any of the grains grown by a farmer, including barley, wheat
  and corn

corn flour
  corn starch

Cornish pasty
  (pronounced *pas-tee*) half-moon shaped pastry, crimped along
  the curved side and filled with ground beef or diced mutton,
  diced potatoes, onion, and sometimes other vegetables

CHEERS

Cheers is the usual salutation when raising a glass. But
in other circumstances it means 'thanks' or 'goodbye' –
context is everything.

courgette
(pronounced *caw-zhet* – the 'g' is pronounced like the 's' in pleasure) zucchini

cream cracker
white unsalted cracker

cream tea
a special 'tea' at which tea is served with bread or scones, clotted cream and jam. This is known as a Devonshire tea in many English-speaking countries, but not in England (except of course in Devon).

SWEETIE, DARLING?

In Britain, candy is called sweets or sweeties, and candy bars are referred to as chocolate bars. If you want to buy a sucker, forget it. You'll have to make that a lollipop.

crisps
potato chips

crumpets
a kind of light bread resembling a muffin, often toasted. Similar to what are known elsewhere as 'English muffins'.

Devonshire tea
see cream tea

double cream
whipping/heavy cream

fish fingers
strips of something resembling fish covered in breadcrumbs, usually bought frozen

FOOD & DRINK

gammon
ham, in the sense of a 'ham steak' on a dinner menu, rather than a thin slice of breakfast ham

gateau
(pronounced *gat-oh*) a rich layer cake, especially one with cream or fruit

greasy spoon
cheap café

haggis
a Scottish dish of ground meat or offal mixed with oatmeal, pepper and salt, all baked or boiled in a sheep's or pig's intestine

high tea
light mid-afternoon meal consisting of tea served with cakes, sandwiches, scones or shortbread. Originally a Scottish institution.

ice lolly
flavoured ice on a stick

icing
frosting

icing sugar
powdered sugar

jam
jelly

jelly
gelatin dessert, often poured into a mould to set

joint
cut of meat used for roasting

kipper
smoked herring

lollipop
sucker

marrow
  white, fleshy, edible gourd

pickle
  any of a variety of thick, vinegary condiments containing
  vegetables and/or fruit. Since the British don't think of this as a
  small pickled cucumber, they don't speak of 'a' pickle – one
  singular pickle. They speak of pickle as a substance, like soup or
  oatmeal. (Would you like some pickle?) They spread it on a
  sandwich or spoon it onto their plates and eat it with their food.

pips
  seeds found in fruit

plaice
> a flat-fish, frequently included on menus, served boned and often in breadcrumbs

ploughman's lunch
> thick slices of bread and cheese with a lettuce salad

pork and apple pie
> pork, onions and apples covered with potato purée and baked in an oven

porridge
> oatmeal

potted pork
> dried pork slowly cooked in a covered saucepan, then mashed and shredded and made into a spread

pudding
> can mean anything from a thick spoonable dessert such as butterscotch or chocolate pudding, a steamed cake, a fluffy pancake or a sausage, to a general word for desserts.
>
> Black pudding comes in a sausage skin and is known in other countries as 'blood sausage'. The British version has a higher content of meal, or filler, and doesn't melt apart in the pan when fried.
>
> Plum pudding, or Christmas pudding, is a dome-shaped cake with fruit, nuts, and sometimes brandy or rum, steamed rather than baked, and cut into slices with a knife.
>
> Yorkshire pudding can be classed as a sort of pancake, baked instead of pan fried. It's made by pouring a batter into a flat pan or iron frying pan and putting it in the oven. It rises high and fluffy all around the edge and in little round peaks in the middle. It's eaten before or with the main meal, topped with gravy.
>
> Puddings is sometimes also used to head the dessert section on a menu.

pulses
  edible seeds of leguminous plants, such as beans, peas and lentils

salad cream
  a type of salad dressing. Salad cream isn't generally offered in restaurants – the British tend to eat their salads plain.

savoury
  having a flavour that isn't sweet, such as a salty, herbal or sour. In other words, a dish is said to be either sweet or savoury

scampi
  a species of shrimp (not the prepared, rich Italian shrimp dish)

scone
  a biscuit-like pastry that goes well with tea

shepherd's pie
  a two-layered oven dish with a ground beef and onion mixture on the bottom and mashed potatoes on the top. Though it's called a pie, there's no crust.

single cream
  coffee cream or light cream

sorbet
  sherbet (the frozen dessert)

spotted dick
  this sounds like a contagious disease, but it's really a dessert consisting of a suet pudding with currants and raisins

spring onion
  scallion

spring roll
  egg roll (the Chinese dish)

FOOD & DRINK

starter

what people call an *hors d'œuvre* in France, an *antipasto* in Italy, a *Vorspeise* in Germany, and an 'appetizer' in the US, they call a starter in Britain

streaky bacon

bacon with meat and fat in strips, rather than meat at the centre and fat around the edge. Most streaky bacon in Britain comes with rind and bone on each slice, and they're a nuisance to cut away. You can buy 'rindless' bacon, but at a higher price.

swedes

yellow turnips; rutabagas

tea

evening meal; supper

tin

can. In Britain, you don't buy a can of peas or beans or stewed tomatoes, you buy a tin

toad in the hole

pork sausages in a pancake mix

tomato sauce

tomato ketchup

DID YOU KNOW ...

The word whisky is a shortened form of whiskybae, or usquebae, which comes from Scottish Gaelic *uisge beatha* – literally meaning 'water of life'.

treacle
  molasses or dark syrup

trifle
  a popular dessert made from a mixture of sponge cake,
  whipped cream, custard, gelatin, fruit and sherry or spirit

Worcestershire sauce
  (pronounced *wus-ter-sher*) sauce made from, among other
  things, anchovies, chillies, garlic and molasses, introduced to
  Britain from Bengal during Victorian times

FOOD & DRINK

DRINKS

In Britain the term a drink means any ingestible liquid – if
someone asks you if you'd like a drink, they may well mean a
cup of tea.

The British use little or no ice in their drinks. In pubs, a small
bucket of ice is usually kept at the bar, but it's not enough for
everyone in the place to have their glass filled with ice at each
order – so settle for a couple of cubes.

If you travel in the summer (and it can get hot in Britain) and
you stay at B&Bs, they mightn't keep ice on hand. If you like a
cold drink, pack an ice cube tray.

Non-Alcoholic

cordial
  sweetened fruit drink

lemonade
  lemon-flavoured carbonated soft drink – *not* freshly
  squeezed lemon juice, water and sugar

'white or black'
  with milk or black? This is the British way of asking how
  you'd like your tea or coffee. Unfortunately, this handy phrase
  doesn't take into account whether or not you'd like sugar.

At the Pub

Pubs are one of the most distinctive contributions the British have made to urban life. They're as cosy as your living room, carpeted, wall-papered, and well furnished. People generally have a favourite pub near their home that they call their local. In villages and small towns it's a place for neighbours to gather and chat. Traditionally, the local has been at the hub of the community, with people treating pubs as virtual extensions of their home, and this tradition is still very much alive in parts of Britain.

Inner-city pubs have a different feel from their country cousins. In country pubs the atmosphere is quiet and laid-back. They're generally friendly, although depending on which part of the country you're in, sometimes you get the feeling somebody is about to warn you to 'beware the moors'. On the other hand, London pubs are all hustle and bustle. Amid the clouds of tobacco smoke and stacks of empty pint glasses there's a frenetic sense of excitement, tinged with desperation. One of the great things about London pubs is their internationalism – between the staff and the patrons, most of the world's accents are represented. But being called a wanker by someone with a Japanese accent just doesn't seem to fit.

The archaic closing time all over England and Wales of 11 pm was introduced for rationing purposes during WWI. On Sundays, most pubs open from noon to 3 pm and from 7 to 10.30 pm, though some stay open all day. A warning bell is rung 10 or 15 minutes before closing so you can make a last trip to the bar. In Scotland, you can drink well into the early morning and all day on Sunday.

SIZE MATTERS

Never ask for just a 'beer', always specify the quantity, such as 'a half of lager' or 'a pint of Guinness'.

Drinks are ordered and paid for at the bar – although in some pubs they may be carried to your table, particularly if ordered with food. And ask at the bar what kind of crisps (potato chips) they have – they'll blow you away with the selection.

bevvy
    an alcoholic drink

free house
    pub that doesn't belong to a brewery, thus is 'free' to sell any brewer's beer

go for a pint
    go for a beer (Let's go for a pint after work tonight.)

licensed trade
    pub or tavern keeping

off-licence/offie
    shop that sells alcohol to go. When you buy alcohol at a shop, you're buying it 'off' the premises where the liquor trade is licenced.

pub
    short for public house – a bar which usually offers food and sometimes accommodation

CHOOSING A 'LOCAL'

If you spend any time in Britain then you need a local. Choosing one can be as simple as getting a comfortable feeling when walking through the door, or friendly bar staff, or the place you meet your mates for a couple after work. Whatever the reason, 'going down the pub' should feel as natural as kicking back in your favourite chair in front of the fire in your own living room.

FOOD & DRINK

publican
    tavern keeper

to shout
    to buy a round of drinks.
    If someone says it's your
    shout, they mean that it's
    your round.

snug
    small, enclosed area in a
    pub which seats only a
    few people

tied house
    pub which is limited to selling the products of one particu-
    lar brewery, thus making it 'tied' to that brewer

> **NAME YOUR POISON**
>
> When a bartender asks what kind of beer you want, you have to say bitter, lager or stout. The potency of beer varies between 2% and 8% – the stronger brews are usually specials or extras.

Wine

> Many pubs display handpainted signs with the words, 'Fine wines'. This could be read as a coded warning that their wine is undrinkable. The general thinking seems to be that anyone who asks for wine in a pub is an outcast and should therefore be served poison. If you want wine, go to a wine bar.
>
> S. Burgen

Spirits

There isn't a wide array of 'cocktails' in Britain. They offer gin
and tonic and vodka and lime, but beyond that, the drinks
are fairly basic – such as whisky or brandy served neat (straight
up) or with water or soft drink.

In pubs, spirits are served in mean-spirited measures laughably called singles and doubles. A single is invisible and its presence can only be detected by sniffing the glass. A double whisky can generally be observed through a powerful electron microscope.

S. Burgen

FOOD & DRINK

blended whisky
mixture of malt and grain whiskies

malt whisky
made from malted barley and usually distilled for 10 to 12 years, up to 21 years

martini
a small glass of dry vermouth (a wine flavoured with herbs). To many visitors, a martini is a cocktail made with gin and dry vermouth, in the proportions of five or so to one. A 'dry' martini has the merest dash of vermouth. If this is what you want, you'll have to make yourself clear.

neat
straight or straight up – not mixed with water or soft drink

vodka and lime
vodka gimlet

grain whisky
mainly used in blends. Made from unmalted corn and malted barley.

single malt
a whisky from a particular area in Scotland

FOOD & DRINK

BEER WARS

Years ago, the 'Great British Boozer' was given its last rites. The Empire of big national breweries swept across the land gobbling up independent brewers and seducing beer drinkers. Traditional cask beers were replaced with fizzy keg beers made at giant beer factories, leaving a thirsty public with few choices. By the mid-70s, all looked lost for the traditional pint, a heady unpasteurised brew left unchilled in the cask. But amid the chaos emerged a brave few who fought back. The Campaign for Real Ale (CAMRA) started a grass roots rebellion. And through tireless work, and despite the rigours of carrying large beer bellies, the complete takeover of the drinking public was held at bay. Today the number of mid-sized independent breweries is hovering around 40, with pub and small breweries topping 200.

These independents represent the frontline between a public with a sophisticated palate demanding quality pubs, and the attempts by some brewing companies to continually try to introduce brewed under licence brand name beers and build pubs that look like something from the Disney Corporation. Although 85% of beer in Britain is still brewed by only four companies, new laws forced them to sell off more than 10,000 pubs, opening up competition and kick-starting an industry that had become all too complacent.

The British spend practically their whole adult lives in pubs, and they want variety. The brewery shake-up allowed independent and small breweries to introduce more choices and better quality beers. While Britain's pubs and inns continue to reinvent themselves, either by harking back to tradition or introducing modern designs, the beer-drinking public has rediscovered the pub as an extension of the home, and pubs in Britain have become almost as integral to life as breathing itself.

D. McKinlay

Cider

scrumpy
> potent cider originally made in England's West Country. Many pubs serve it straight from the barrel.

snake bite
> mix of half cider and half lager, with a dash of black-currant cordial

Beer

ale
> milder, sweeter and darker than beer. Generally drunk at room temperature.

bitter
> strong beer with a relatively high alcohol content, served at cellar temperature to enhance the flavour

FOOD & DRINK

FOOD & DRINK

lager
> more carbonated than bitter, and served colder than other types of beer. Lager and bitter are generally lighter in colour than ale and stout.

lager top
> pint or glass of beer topped with a large dash of lemonade

pint
> pint of beer (roughly half a litre). In British pubs, beer is usually ordered by the pint. If you don't want a whole pint, ask for a half pint.

shandy
> a popular drink in which beer and lemonade are mixed together – a bit astonishing to some visitors

stout
> dark, full-bodied beer made from malt

PUB NAMES

Pub names have a long history in Britain, although relatively few are unique. They started during the Middle Ages, when most people were illiterate, as roughly painted pictures used as signs. Today, with more than 55,000 pubs, the list of names is long. They often reflect an event, a person or even an attitude. The Bunker's Knob was named after the 'bonking' or banging noise made by the club foot of a parish constable when he walked. Mother Huff Cap refers to a 16th century term for strong beer. Drinking such strong ale 'huff's ones cap', or makes you think you're the centre of the universe. The Olde Tippling Philosopher refers to the drinking habits of Plato and Socrates, while Sixteen String Jack is named after an 18th century highwayman who wore eight coloured strings around each knee of his breeches. A lover of fine clothes, he's said to have gone to the gallows in a new pea-green suit.

D. McKinlay

ENTERTAINMENT

SHOPPING

Many shops now open on Sundays in Britain, and large supermarkets are now staying open untill 9 or 10 pm.

car boot sale

> sale of old or unused household items. This is similar to the 'garage sales' or 'rummage sales' people hold in their drive-ways, except the car boot sale ostensibly operates out of the back of a car or van. In reality, however, people actually haul their stuff out of the car and put it on tables and on the ground. These sales generally take place in car parks, with a group of people selling their second-hand things.

chemist

> pharmacy. The chemist in Britain is the place to get prescription and non-prescription drugs. You can also, in many cases, have film developed there, and can usually buy perfume, cosmetics, soap and items you'd find in the 'lotions' and 'toiletries' departments of larger stores. However, you won't find things such as fuses, magazines, greeting cards, stationery supplies or potato chips except in the large chain chemists.

> Chemists generally close between 5 and 6 pm. Most towns and even villages usually designate one chemist to stay open a little longer, but you won't necessarily know which one that is. Grocery stores in Britain generally don't carry a wide range of non-prescription drugs (although many larger supermarkets have a pharmacy section), so if you want a particular anti-histamine or sleep aid or some such thing, you'll have to get to the chemist before 6 pm when it closes for the evening.

fiver
  five pound note

custom
  business/patronage. In Britain you hear phrases like, 'They
  get a lot of custom in that shop' or 'I won't give him my
  custom any more'.

greengrocer
  vegetable store or market, and, in some villages,
  someone who goes from house-to-house in their lorry
  selling vegetables

ironmongery
  hardware store

Marks and Sparks
  nickname for one of the most popular department stores in
  Britain, Marks & Spencer.

p
  pence

paying desk
  the sales counter or cash register in a department store
  or shop

quid
  one pound sterling

stationer
  stationery store

London Markets

Brick Lane
  held in the East End, on the streets off Brick Lane and along
  Bethnal Green Rd. Offers a diverse range of goods such as
  gold, antique books and dodgy furniture.

ENTERTAINMENT

Brixton

cosmopolitan market with plenty of exotic foods and Jamaican music along with wigs, homeopathic root cures and rare records. Held in Electric Ave and Granville Arcade.

Camden

consists of hundreds of stalls which virtually extend from Camden Town tube station to Chalk Farm tube station

Petticoat Lane

Sunday street market held in the East End, between Aldgate and Bishopsgate. Good buys include second-hand clothing, cheap jewellery and fruit.

DID YOU KNOW ... Highland games take place throughout summer in Scotland, and involve piping and dancing competitions and sporting events. Originally, the games were organised by clan chiefs and kings who'd recruit the strongest competitors for their armies or as bodyguards. Events which test the strength of participants include tossing the caber, which involves heaving a tree trunk into the air, throwing the hammer and putting the stone.

ENTERTAINMENT

Portobello Road

popular street market found just northwest of Kensington Gardens, stretching from Notting Hill to Ladbroke Grove. The selection on offer includes hand-made jewellery, paintings, second-hand clothing, antiques, bric-a-brac and fruit and vegetables.

Clothes

anorak

hooded, weatherproof jacket. The word comes via Danish from Inuit, in which it meant a hooded, sealskin garment designed for polar temperatures. The British have adopted the word and the jacket into their culture, though theirs is a lighter version, made of cloth rather than sealskin.

balaclava

close-fitting head and neck covering which may cover the face as well, leaving holes for the eyes and mouth. Used as a hooded mask or ski mask. You probably won't have use for this word unless you're planning to rob a bank. The word was adopted in Victorian times when British women made head coverings for soldiers fighting in the frigid winter in the city of Balaclava, in the Ukraine during the Crimean War.

braces

suspenders for trousers

dressing gown

bath robe. The British use the term dressing gown not only for the silky garment you can lounge around the house in, but for terry cloth robes as well.

fancy dress

if you're invited to a fancy dress party in Britain, you're supposed to come in your Tarzan get-up or your Dracula cape, not just your pink chiffon

flip flops
 thongs (the footwear)

frock
 dress

jumper
 sweater

knickers
 women's underpants

mackintosh/mac
 raincoat

pants
 underwear

suspender
 garter (strip of elastic attached to a girdle or garter belt to
 hold stockings up)

MORRIS DANCING

For all its clichéd absurdity, Morris dancing holds some popularity in England. While nobody seems sure of its origin, it's believed to be an ancient fertility ritual. Women aren't allowed take part, a tradition enforced by the Morris Ring, the unofficial governing body of the dance. If you want to see men dressed in white, waving bells and hankies, and prancing about with their dignity around their ankles, then there's an annual display in the village of Bampton in Oxfordshire every Whit Sunday (the seventh Sunday after Easter) to welcome the summer.

M. Hughes

ENTERTAINMENT

tights
> nylon pantyhose. Stockings that attach to a garter belt have always been called stockings both in Britain and the US. But when the one-piece garment that covers the legs and lower torso came onto the market, Americans called them 'pantyhose', while the British called them tights.

trainers
> gym/tennis/jogging shoes

trousers
> this is the word for both men's and women's pants or slacks in Britain. The word pants means underpants.

vest
> short-sleeved or sleeveless undershirt

waistcoat
> vest (the close fitting, buttoned garment often worn under a jacket). The most common pronunciation in London and the southern parts of England is exactly as it looks, *waist-coat*. An older pronunciation of the word, more common in northern England, is *wes-kit*.

wellies
> high rubber boots. These are named after the Duke of Wellington (1769-1852), the great general and statesman who defeated Napoleon in the Battle of Waterloo. The high, handsome boots, covering the knee in front and cut away behind, became one of Wellington's trademarks. Today, they usually mean rubber boots that reach the knee.

THEATRE

booking office
> ticket office. The general term to book is used in Britain when reserving tickets or a table at a restaurant or when ordering a cab in advance. So you book a table and you book a cab and so on.

in the gods
> in the upper balconies. If someone sells you tickets to a play
> at one of the West End theatres, and they tell you your seats
> are in the gods, take your binoculars.

Globe Theatre
> the original Globe Playhouse was built in 1598-99 and
> closed down 26 years after Shakespeare's death in 1642.
> In 1997, a replica opened 200 yards from the Globe's
> original location. It reflects the original as closely as possible
> with performances taking place under open sky in daylight
> or simulated daylight, and with standing room for 500
> (as well as seating on wooden benches for 1000). Plays by
> Shakespeare and his contemporaries are performed from
> May to September.

pantomime
> during the Christmas season in Britain, a favourite form of
> entertainment is the pantomime. It's a theatrical performance
> in which a fairy tale or nursery story is dramatised with
> music and dancing. Though it may seem that these productions
> are for children, they're attended by people of all ages. They
> *aren't* done in mime.

Royal National Theatre
> England's flagship theatre which showcases both
> contemporary plays and classics, as well as hosting young
> international companies. Its three auditoria are located on
> London's South Bank.

stalls
> orchestra seats in a theatre

West End
> theatre district in west London where you can see the
> world's best in drama, comedy and musicals (analogous to
> Broadway). People in the know who want discounted tickets
> go to the discount booking office in Leicester Square, in the
> heart of the theatre district.

ENTERTAINMENT

ENTERTAINMENT

MUSIC

Britain has had an enormous impact on the evolution of pop music worldwide, redefining itself one decade after another. Beginning in the 60s, The Beatles put Britain on the pop map when they stormed the world with their cheeky Liverpudlian charm and timeless melodies. They were followed by a multitude of groups led by The Rolling Stones, The Who and The Kinks – all pioneers in their own way. Sir Cliff Richard, Britain's squeaky-clean version of Elvis, had sprung up a few years earlier (and like a malfunctioning jack-in-the-box, he's been springing up ever since).

In the 70s, British pop fans were stretched to breaking point between two extremes. Glam rock went head-to-head with punk – while the Mods had revived and were spoiling for a fight on the sidelines. Their respective fans often took the rhetoric literally, but each genre left a lasting impression on Britain and its music scene. Glam boys David Bowie, Marc Bolan and Bryan Ferry swapped cosmetics and glitter. The Clash flew the punk flag all the while that Sid Vicious and The Sex Pistols were beating the shit out of anyone who didn't care for their brand of anarchism. Deep Purple, Led Zeppelin and Genesis couldn't decide which camp they belonged to, so forged their own way.

The 80s witnessed the arrival of the New Romantics. Duran Duran, ABC, Spandau Ballet and later Wham represented this stylised scene and brought quiffs back into fashion. (Look through any 30-something's photo album and, at some stage,

MUSIC

they'll say, 'Yeah, that was my New Romantic phase'.) The Police were disowned by punks for having talent, while UB40 sold lots of their wishy-washy white reggae. Angst came into vogue later that decade with Morrissey brilliantly whining at the forefront with his band, The Smiths. Poet Billy Bragg constantly pricked the nation's consciousness while personifying a thorn in the side of Margaret Thatcher's Greed Society.

In the 90s, dance music came overground while hanging on to the credibility of the bunkers. What was known as Dance branched off into so many different forms like techno, house, jungle, garage, handbag, industrial, acid and hip-hop that heads were spinning even before the club drugs kicked in. While the British music scene was catching its breath, it was mugged by American grunge, à la Kurt Cobain (Nirvana) and other badly dressed geniuses.

Post-grunge brought Britpop, the quintessential sound of British Indie (independent) music. While the British music press decreed Britpop a thing of the past, they were plastering it on their front covers. And the word Indie itself is a misnomer, as the major record labels control the scene more than ever. The late 90s saw Blur, Oasis and Pulp as the leading exponents of this genre and seminal Britpop albums include Oasis' *(What's the Story) Morning Glory*, Blur's *Parklife* and Pulp's *Different Class*. Or you could just buy Rialto's *Rialto* which is a good composite of all three. A common thread to Britpop is whistleable tunes and simple lyrics, along the lines

MUSIC

of The Beatles. Indeed, the brains behind Oasis, Noel Gallagher, freely admits the debt owed to Liverpool's fab four. So, you could say that British music has come full circle.

Dance and electronic seem to be the future. Trip-hop, a mutated drug-inspired branch of dance, is flourishing with brilliant atmospheric sounds and darkly poetic lyrics. Massive Attack, Portishead and Tricky (all from Bristol) are the originals.

Boy bands, manufactured by record companies and marketing gurus, have been gigantically popular in the last decade with Take That getting as big as an average bunch of blokes could possibly get before eventually bursting, breaking up and following solo careers. Now, girl bands have taken over with the Spice Girls blandifying the world with their effervescent brand of girl power.

While the British can be pretty insular about their music and their tastes, Britain is one of the world centres for pop music, with Manchester ('Madchester' in indie parlance) as its creative studio and London as its gallery. In some ways Britain is in between genres at the moment, with Britpop already having peaked. But in the meantime, it's still pumping out some of the best pop music in the world and the joy for the visitor to London is that, on any night of the week, you can see brilliant bands down at your local venue. Check *Time Out* in London and regional listings for details.

M. Hughes

FESTIVALS

Britain hosts a plethora of festivals each summer. Catering for a wide range of tastes, they offer the best local and international acts.

Chelsea Flower Show
> held at the Royal Hospital, Chelsea, in the last week of May

Edinburgh International Festival
> one of the world's largest and most important arts festivals, the International Festival is held between mid-August and early September

Fleadh
> annual festival of traditional and contemporary Irish music held in Finsbury Park, North London in June

Fringe Festival
> held concurrently with the International Festival in Edinburgh, the Fringe Festival offers hundreds of amateur and professional avante garde performances

Glastonbury
> held in the West Country near Bath, Glastonbury is a muddy institution in the tradition of Woodstock but with younger, less likely hipfolk. Practically everyone, artists included, camp out for three days, and drop out for the duration with lots of New Age frivolity.

London Pride
> Europe's largest gay and lesbian march and festival, held in late June

Military Tattoo
> running for three weeks from early August, the Edinburgh Military Tattoo coincides with the International Festival

T in the Park
> Glasgow rocks to T in the Park, one of the best annual festivals in Britain

ENTERTAINMENT

Phoenix Festival
: multi-genre festival with at least five different stages filled by various musicians over five days. It takes place on a deserted air-strip in Stratford-upon-Avon, just outside Birmingham, in July.

Tribal Gathering
: the festival season usually kicks off in June with Tribal Gathering, an enormous dance party as close to London as the organisers are permitted to get. If you're into the dance culture and the club-in-a-field lifestyle, this is the ideal place to hear Britain's best spinmeisters and live dance bands.

Virgin Festival
: known as V99, V2000 and so on, this two-day festival is relatively new, has several stages and is held outside London

USEFUL TERMS

Auntie
: endearing though dated term for the BBC

beefeater
: yeoman warder of the Tower of London who enacts the Ceremony of the Keys, which involves locking the tower gates and depositing the keys at the Queen's residence. Beefeaters also give guided tours of the Tower. The name dates back to the 17th century when the warders were given a daily ration of the luxury item beef, and beer.

concession
: discount. If you go to the movies and there's a sign in the window advertising concessions, it isn't referring to a concessions stand where you can buy popcorn and chocolate bars. It's referring to the fact that you can get a discount on your ticket if you're a senior citizen, a student, and so on.

Guy Fawkes Day
    firework and bonfire celebrations are held throughout
    Britain on 5 November to commemorate an attempted
    Catholic coup

Speakers' Corner
    every Sunday, members of the public have the opportunity
    to test their oratory skills in Hyde Park, London (near
    Marble Arch), a tradition begun in the 19th century in
    response to local riots

ENTERTAINMENT

the Proms

series of Promenade Concerts held annually. They're televised live-to-air from the Royal Albert Hall in London by the BBC and relayed to a large crowd via screens in Hyde Park. The Last Night of the Proms, held in late summer, brings out a patriotic fervour which peaks at the finale *Land of Hope and Glory*. The Proms have nothing to do with high school dances.

theme park

amusement park

trailers

previews. If this doesn't confuse visitors to Britain, nothing will. The 'previews' in British cinemas are called trailers and the term to trail means to preceed or come before something. No problem.

If you want to take a shortcut into the heart of British culture, watch the British at play. They're fierce and passionate about their sport, whether participating or watching.

The mood of the nation is more closely aligned to the success of its international teams in major competition than the Exchequer's forecasts or even the weather. Britain proudly gave the world many of its most popular games including football, rugby and golf, but it's a sore point that the world took these sports and became better at them than the creators themselves. Having said that, Britain is a world power in the sports arena. It hosts numerous premier events annually and, no matter when you visit, there'll be an event taking place that will seem to preoccupy the population.

London hosts a myriad of these sporting events and if you want to see live action, there's a full weekly sporting events calendar in *Time Out* magazine.

FOOTBALL

You may know this game as 'soccer' but calling it such won't win friends with the locals.

Football is by far the most popular sport in Britain and was invented in England, probably in the 12th century, when unruly mobs played with scant regard for any semblance of rules. Despite repeated Royal bans, the game grew in popularity and several hundred years later the Football Association was founded and the formal rules of the contemporary game were adopted.

FOOTBALL CHANTS

When the referee ... eh, makes an unpopular decision.
The referee's a wanker!

The term 'soccer' is believed to have been coined by a public school boy in the 1880s. It was – and still is – the common practice of public school boys to abbreviate words while adding 'er' to the end. When asked if he wanted to play rugger (rugby) the student said he'd rather play soccer, a curious abbreviation of 'association' (the rules of the then recently established Football Association).

Disregarding the notorious offside rule (which nearly every newcomer to the game has difficulty grasping), football is relatively straightforward. There are 11 players on each team and five players (substitutes) on the bench. Up to three subs can be brought into the game at any stage to replace any of the original 11. The aim is to get the round-shaped ball into the opposition's goal while defending your own. Players are allowed to use any part of their body except their hands and arms to block or control the ball, but only the feet and head are used for striking it. Matches are made up of two 45-minute halves and a 15-minute interval in between. Although it's clearly a contact sport, players aren't allowed to push, grab, tug, strike or kick opponents and must only target the ball in tackles or contests.

Football's a very low scoring game compared to most other sports. No-score draws are reasonably commonplace and, in fact, these games are sometimes considered entertaining. It's this boring statistic which has, on the face of it, prevented the game taking off in the US. To make the game more

SPORT

FOOTBALL CHANTS

You may hear them chant:

What a load of rubbish ...

Or when the crowd wants to tease someone about being overweight:

Who ate all the pies,
Who ate all the pies,
You fat bastard,
You fat bastard,
You ate all the pies.

FOOTBALL CHANTS

Each club has its own song or chant. The following is a favourite at South London team Crystal Palace, which spends most of its time in the first division challenging for promotion to the Premiership.

Ee-I ee-I ee-I O
Up the football league we go
When we win promotion
This is what we sing
We are Palace, super Palace
Top of the football league.

appealing to Americans, moves to increase the level of scoring in each game have been suggested, such as increasing the size of the target or goal – although any such tinkering with the rules would be seen as contamination by most of the football world.

English football found itself in the doldrums in the 90s when crowd violence led to declining attendances and a ban from European competition. This, combined with two stadia disasters which cost the lives of 140 fans, spoiled the general public's appetite for the game.

However, in the last decade, football has gone through a revolution and has made a serious comeback thanks to slick marketing off the pitch and foreign flair on it. Working class author Nick Hornby set the ball rolling, so to speak, with his brilliant book *Fever Pitch* in the early 90s. These memoirs of a soccer fanatic brought credibility back to football – it even became hip – and soon the stands were packed again. Most people in Britain now support a football team, be they cultured season-ticket holders, kids begging Santa Claus for the latest Manchester United kit, or new supporters surreptitiously scanning the newspaper to check their team's form.

The season runs from August to May, and if you fancy catching a game some Saturday afternoon there's sure to be one on nearby.

SPORT

The Positions

Teams play various formations to get the best result out of each game. Basically there are defenders, midfielders and attackers (or strikers). The goalkeeper is always in the same position. A standard formation is 4.4.2 which means there are four defenders, four midfielders and two strikers. A more attacking formation, for example, would be 3.5.2 where the team decides to play only three defenders and an extra midfielder to put more pressure on the opposition's goal. There are many intricacies within these general rules but you'll only learn them by watching the game.

The Football League

The English league comprises four divisions. The Premier League is the top league, followed by the first, second and third divisions.

Go to a football match. For the full cultural monty, don't go to see Liverpool or Manchester United, go to a match in a lower division, say Grimsby Town vs Hartlepool. The players will all be English and most of them won't be much good. They'll be playing in a bleak stadium on a surface slightly smoother than a sheep meadow and you can keep yourself warm with cups of squirrel-grey tea (no relation to Earl Grey).

You'll be in the company of between three and eight thousand passionate fans, who are third and fourth generation supporters of their teams. As a Grimsby Town supporter remarked, without a trace of irony, 'Anyone can support Man United, they're a great team, they've got great players. But to support a club like Grimsby Town, now that's what English football is all about, because you know they're crap, and they always were crap, and they haven't got any money so they're going to stay crap'.

S. Burgen

After each season the teams who finish bottom of each league get relegated to the next lower division, and the teams who finish top get promoted to the next level.

Major Teams

There are enormous differences between the resources and support enjoyed by some clubs in the Premier League and those in the lower divisions. In fact, often giants play alongside minnows in the same division. The biggest club, and the most successful, of the last decade is Manchester United and it's virtually impossible to get a ticket to see them play at home these days. Because they've been so dominant, the fans from practically every other team love to hate 'Man U'. The biggest teams, their nicknames and their home grounds, include:

Arsenal	(The Gunners)	Highbury, London
Chelsea	(The Blues)	Stamford Bridge, London
Liverpool	(The Reds)	Anfield
Manchester United	(The Red Devils)	Old Trafford
Newcastle United	(The Magpies)	St James Park

The Scottish League

Scotland has a separate, smaller league structured in the same way as England's. The teams from England and Scotland don't play any domestic competitive games against one another but occasionally meet in European competition.

Two teams from Glasgow – Celtic and Rangers – have dominated this league since its inception in 1874. The battle between the two teams is commonly known as the Old Firm. The roots of this intense rivalry stem from the Catholic–Protestant political struggle, with Celtic representing the Catholic community and Rangers the Protestant. While the sectarian and often violent nature of this rivalry has little to do with football, fans from Glasgow are among the most passionate of any in the sporting world.

Rangers won nine consecutive titles before Celtic stopped their run in 1998. Celtic play at Celtic Park, and Rangers at Ibrox.

Major Annual Events

The season climaxes in May with the FA Cup final at Wembley Stadium, in North London. This is the oldest football competition in the world where, with a good run, amateur teams could get the opportunity to scalp the likes of Manchester United. Such romantic notions are at the cornerstone of the competition.

A smaller League Cup competition concludes in March and is only open to teams in the Premiership and Football League.

The Charity Shield matches the winners of the Premier League and the FA Cup in the first event of the following season. The Shield is played in August at Wembley Stadium, the fortress of English football.

England's International Team

Despite the fact that England pioneered the professional game and showed the rest of the world how to play, it has just one World Cup victory (1966) to its credit. Despite the lack of international success, everyone involved in English football – from the fans to the media – still has a disproportionate sense of its own importance in international terms. The country gets so pent up about its prospects in major tournaments that when the inevitable defeat comes, heads roll (usually the manager's).

FOOTBALL CHANTS

You're going to get your fucking heads kicked in!
Pretty self-explanatory.

Que sera sera
Whatever will be will be,
We're going to Wem-be-ley
Que sera sera.

A FEW BIG NAMES

David Beckham
Tremendously gifted midfield player with a dodgy temperament and a nice haircut. Became the most unpopular man in England when he got sent off in the World Cup finals in France in 1998. England lost the game and were subsequently eliminated from the competition.

Michael Owen
The revelation of recent years, Owen made his England debut in 1998 aged 17 and became one of the sensations of that year's World Cup. Brilliant player with natural goalscoring instinct much prized by his club. His image adorns the bedroom walls of teenage girls and boys alike.

Alan Shearer
England's captain and star player of the 1990s, Shearer is lightning quick, deadly with his head and can score goals with either foot. He's a Geordie (from Newcastle) and set what was then a world transfer record of £15 million when he moved from Blackburn Rovers back to his home team of Newcastle United in 1997.

Paul Gascoigne
The most popular player of his generation, 'Gazza', the quintessential English 'lad', was blessed with undoubted genius and the ability to win matches on his own. He was one of the most skilful players to come out of Britain but never reached his full potential on the pitch because of his hedonism off it. Now past his peak, Gazza has also played in both the Italian and Scottish Leagues.

SPORT

Scotland's International Team

Scotland has a good record at reaching the final stages of major international tournaments. But once there, the team doesn't tend to do much apart from spring the odd upset. Scotland gets more attention for the jovial, drinking spirit of its travelling fans (the Tartan Army) than for the team's exploits on the pitch. Scotland plays its home games at Hampden Park.

Wales' International Team

Wales has no professional domestic competition of its own, and it's main teams play in the English Football League. The valleys have been the breeding ground for some of Britain's most flamboyantly gifted players, particularly prolific attacking players like Ryan Giggs,

---

FOOTBALL CHANTS

The fans from London clubs chant this – to the tune of *Guantanamera* – when they're playing practically any team not from London:

Sheep shagging bastards,
You're only sheep shagging bastards,
Sheep shagging bastards,
You're only sheep shagging bastards.

Manchester United fans used to sing (to the tune of *Jesus Christ Superstar*):

Georgie Best
Superstar
How many goals have you scored so far?

The fans from any team playing against Manchester United used to sing:

Georgie Best
Superstar
Wears frilly knickers and a Playtex bra.

Ian Rush and Mark Hughes. The national team consistently features world class players but, as it relies on too many average ones to make up the numbers, it has enjoyed little success internationally.

booking
> when a player commits a serious foul he's shown a yellow card. If a player gets two yellow cards he's then shown the red card and expelled from the game. If the foul is serious enough, the player may be shown the red card without getting an initial warning.

cross
> a ball across the face of the goal is a cross

dive
> players often take a dive to give the impression that they've been fouled so the referee will award them a free kick or penalty

half-time
> interval

header
> when a player strikes the ball with his head

kick-off
> the start of the game

man on
> when he (the team-mate) has the ball and is about to be challenged

offside
> complicated rule involving a player being in an illegal position

---

FOOTBALL CHANTS

Fans may start singing, to the tune of the Dave Clarke Five's *Glad All Over*:

One fan: 'You say that you love me.'
Whole Crowd: 'All of the time.'
One fan: 'You say that you need me.'
Whole Crowd: 'Always be mine ...'
In unison: '... 'cos I'm feeling (stamp, stamp) glad all over, yes I'm (stamp, stamp) glad all over, and I'm feeling (stamp, stamp) glad all over that you're miiiiiiiiinnee.'

over-the-head scissors kick
    a spectacularly skilful play which you probably won't see
    much of in Britain

penalty
    when a player defending his own goal fouls an opponent in
    the penalty box (the area in front of goal) a penalty is
    awarded. This is a free shot against the keeper which is
    usually scored.

referee's assistant
    official name for what everyone calls a linesman

skipper
    the team's captain, normally the one wearing an armband

the spot

> the penalty spot, where the ball is placed for the penalty kick

sweeper

> a defensive position. The player plays behind the normal defensive structure and 'sweeps away' any balls that come through.

RUGBY UNION

There are two different codes of rugby played in Britain – rugby union and rugby league. Rugby union is traditionally the privilege of the middle and upper classes in England and hence, in the language of public school boys, it's commonly known as rugger. Rugby league (see page 138) is predominantly played and supported by the working classes. Both games are equally popular in England, but in Scotland and Wales there's no class division in rugby union so the alternative code of rugby league has had less impact.

Rugby is believed to have originated in 1823 at Rugby School, in Warwickshire, England, when William Ellis picked up the ball and ran with it during a football match. The Rugby Union Association was formally inaugurated in 1871.

There are 15 players on each team. Points are scored when the oval-shaped ball is grounded across the opponent's goal line. The player's hand must be on the ball as it's pressed down for the score to count. This is called a try and is worth four points. After each try, the scoring team is awarded an opportunity to kick a goal (which in this case is called a conversion) from parallel to where the try was scored. If the ball is successfully kicked between the H-shaped posts and above the crossbar, the team is awarded two points. When a goal is scored at any other time in the match it's worth three points.

SPORT

Tackling above the shoulders is prohibited but anywhere else on the body is fair game. The ball may be kicked to someone in front (as long as they've run from behind the player with the ball), or thrown behind to a running team-mate. When a player either deliberately or inadvertently moves the ball forward with his hands, a free ball is awarded to the other team for what is known as a knock on.

> ### FOOTBALL CHANTS
>
> What the fuck, what the fuck,
> What the fucking hell was that?
> What the fuuuucking hell was that?
>
> Usually sung after an opposition player has made a mistake.

Rugby union only went professional in the 1990s and London is the heart of the code in England. Some of the major teams are Harlequins, Richmond, Wasps and London Irish, while elsewhere Bath and Leicester are traditional giants.

Internationals

The most important annual competition is the Six-Nations Tournament, contested by England, Scotland, Wales, Ireland, France and Italy (Ireland's team represents both the Republic and Northern Ireland). Each team plays alternate home and away matches, and plays each of the other teams only once during the competition. The Six-Nations Tournament takes place from February to March and is a big event in the sporting calendar. England plays at least twice a year at Twickenham in London, the shrine of English rugby. Scotland plays at Murrayfield in Edinburgh, and Wales now play at the new Millennium Stadium in Cardiff.

Within the Six-Nations Tournament if one team from the British Isles beats all the others (England, Scotland, Wales and Ireland) it wins the Triple Crown. If any team in the tournament beats all the others, it gets the Grand Slam. The last placed team gets the dreaded Wooden Spoon.

Will Carling captained a highly successful England team through the early 1990s but gained equal recognition for an alleged affair with Princess Diana.

ruck

a ruck takes place when the ball is on the ground and one or more players from each team are on their feet and in physical contact, pushing each other in an attempt to gain ground, like in a scrum

scrum

originally a disordered struggle in which each team attempted to force the ball and opposing players towards the opposing goal. Today it's an organised play meant to accomplish the same thing. A scrum is called when there is an infringement or a breakdown in play. Usually, the team that's going forward gets to put the ball in. The forwards from each team lock arms and put their heads down. The middle player in each front row is known as the hooker and the players on either side of him are the props. The scrum-half puts the ball in when he thinks his team has the momentum and then races around behind his team-mates to gather the ball when they back heel it out of the scrum, and then play continues. It often ends in a great pile-up.

FOOTBALL CHANTS

We're on our way to Wembley,
We shall not be moved.
On our way to Wembley,
We shall not be moved.
Just like a team that's gonna win the FA Cup,
We shall not be moved.

The fans from practically every team sing this after they've had a victory in any round of the FA Cup.

SPORT

RUGBY LEAGUE

League, as it's commonly known, is most popular in the north of England. The rules are similar to rugby union although it's a bit more like the traditional sport of British Bulldogs, where players have to barge their way through a wall of opponents to reach the other side.

League broke away from rugby union in England in the 1890s, when many of the rules changed and it rapidly became semi-professional at top level.

There are 13 players on each team. They attempt to get the oval ball past their opponents

FOOTBALL CHANTS

I'm blind, I'm deaf,
I wanna be a ref.
R e f e r e e e e e e,
refereeeee.

by hand-passing (always backwards) or kicking it (usually forwards, but the receiver must have run from behind the kicker). Grounding the ball beyond the opponents goal line is a try, which is worth four points. A try can be converted, in the same way as in rugby union, for two points. A tackled player regains his feet and heels the ball backwards to a team-mate. After six tackles, the other team gets possession of the ball.

League is played during the summer. The teams to keep an eye out for in the Super League are St Helens, Wigan Warriors and Warrington Wolves.

CRICKET

This quintessentially English game has been played formally since the 18th century. It is, officially, England's national game and its popularity has generally been confined to the countries of the Commonwealth, particularly in the Indian sub-continent and the Antipodes. Traditionally, it was a game for toffs (British slang for the upper-classes) and subsequently was ignored by the masses in Scotland and Wales, although it is played in Wales.

If you're unfamiliar with the rules and have only seen bits and pieces of the game, you may see it as a form of English torture – that if there was ever a need for TV highlights of a game, surely this was it. On the other hand, if you're patient and learn the intricacies of the game, you could find it enriching and wonder how you ever survived without cricket being part of your sporting vocabulary. If you're interested, go to a match with somebody who can explain the rules and shed light on the proceedings, and then soak up the atmosphere.

Basically, it's an open-air sport, played with a ball, bats and wickets. It has some similarities with baseball in the US – though Brits would cringe to hear the comparison.

The Rules

Here we go, in its simplest terms.

At any one time, there are two batsmen on the pitch. While their team is batting they're the only two representatives on the ground. The batsman's aim is to score runs (points). The bowler's aim is to stop them scoring runs and his entire team is spread out across the ground, fielding.

The bowler must bowl the ball with a straight arm, aiming at the batsman's wicket (the stumps he stands in front of). Six balls (an over) are bowled at one of the two sets of stumps. One of the batsmen is on strike (defending the stumps the bowler is aiming at). After these six balls, another bowler bowls the next over at the other set of stumps, at the opposite end.

The bowler tries to get the batsman out or dismissed. The two main ways of doing this are to either hit the stumps or force the batsman to mishit (edge) or strike the ball into the air where a fielder can catch it before it hits the ground. The wicket-keeper, who crouches down directly behind the stumps, is the prime catcher of balls edged in the air. When one batsman is out, he's replaced by a new one. The innings (the team's chance at batting) is over when 10 out of the 11 in the team are out.

A FEW GOOD MEN

Along with England's dismal performances throughout the 1990s, there's also been a dearth of heroes. Therefore, this list is mainly drawn from an earlier era which most English cricket fans would rather celebrate.

Graham Gooch (1975–95)

Gooch holds the record for the most test runs for England (8900 – third highest in the world). He also has the most caps (appearances) for England, despite being banned from test cricket for three years after he led a rebel tour to the then boycotted South Africa.

David Gower (1978–92)

Gower is widely recognised as one of the artists of the game. His unique style was captivating as he amassed over 8000 first class (at top level) runs for England. He was also something of a prankster – on one memorable occasion after he wasn't selected to play in Brisbane, Australia, he flew in a light aircraft over the field of play, 'buzzing' his team-mates during a match.

Ian Botham (1977–92)

before becoming a commentator, Botham was the greatest player of the contemporary game in England. An aggressive fast medium bowler, he had the ability to score runs off any attack, and was a great fielder. His exploits on the field were matched only by his legendary partying off it.

Geoff Boycott (1964–81)

Boycott was the greatest English batsman of his generation, although never the most popular. He was once dropped by England following his highest test innings, 246, due to slow scoring. Controversy was always Boycott's shadow – after retiring as a player he became a celebrated commentator around the world, but in late 1998 a French court gave him a three month suspended sentence for assaulting a former girlfriend and his media contacts suddenly dried up.

When the batsman strikes the ball, he and the other batsman run to each other's end of the pitch (crease). When they reach the opposite crease, one run is scored and they may return for another run immediately, and so on. If the batsmen are running and one of the fielders hits either of the wickets, or stumps, with the ball and dislodges a **bail** (either of two wooden bars placed across the top of the stumps), then the nearest batsman is **run out**. The batsman cannot be run out if his bat is grounded beyond the line marking his crease.

If the batsman strikes the ball and it reaches the boundary (the perimeter of the field of play) he's awarded four runs. If the ball goes over the boundary without bouncing first, he's awarded six runs.

At stumps is the term for the end of the day's play.

The batsmen don't have to attempt to hit each ball bowled to them. Neither do the batsmen have to run each time a ball is struck.

International matches are called tests. One-day games, where each team bats once with a limited number of overs, are gaining popularity. However, one-day games are regarded by puritan cricket fans as travesties of the traditional game where each team gets two innings and the game can last for five days. Even then, these matches often end in draws because neither team has time to force a win. If this is your experience after watching your first five-day test (a) you'll be unlucky and (b) you'll probably never watch it again.

The teams that make up the main domestic competition are drawn from counties (or shires), predominantly from the 'home counties' (south-east of England). This level of competition is known as County Cricket.

Some of the original clubs established in the 18th century

CRICKET GROUNDS

Test matches in England are held at Lords, home of the famous Marlybone Cricket Club, and the Oval, both in London.

still survive today, including the famous Marylebone Cricket Club (MCC) which is based at Lord's in North London, the home of English cricket.

The English team tours each year and hosts at least one tour from one of the other major cricket-playing nations (Australia, India, Pakistan, Sri Lanka, South Africa and the West Indies).

Victory or defeat between England and Australia in test matches is referred to as winning, losing or retaining the Ashes. After a great Australian victory in 1882, there was a mock obituary for English cricket in *The Times*, in which it was said that the 'body' was cremated and the ashes taken to Australia. England and Australia play each other every two years, alternately in each country.

In recent years, England has been thrashed on a regular basis by many of these teams (especially Australia). However, in a nation so passionate about the sport, and so entrenched in its tradition, it's only a matter of time before it bounces back as a cricketing force. You might be there to witness the turning point.

CRICKET CHANTS

A core of flag-waving English fans known as the Barmy Army sing and chant their way through English test matches. One chant includes:

We're so good its unbelievable
(about England, however badly the team is performing)

You're so poor it's unbelievable
(about the opposition, however well they're performing)

SPORT

OTHER SPORTS & GAMES

catapult

    sling-shot

Cluedo

    Clue (the board game)

conkers

a game played by children using horse chestnuts, which are also called conkers. English children have called horse chestnuts conkers since the early 17th century. In this intriguing game, they take the green shell off of a horse chestnut (or conker), thread a string through the nut, knotted on the end to keep the nut from flying off, then take turns swinging their conker at the other person's till one of them breaks.

darts

this is primarily a pub game although during major competitions entire arenas are turned into bars. It's popular throughout Britain and many people play in teams representing their local pubs.

Players throw three darts consecutively, usually aiming for the maximum score which is to have all three darts in the treble 20 bed which leads to the characteristically long drawn out 'One hun-dred and eigggghhhh-tteeee!'. Games start backwards from 501 and the player's score is deducted from this until they can finish on a double (so if a player has 40 left, they aim for double 20). The round bit in the middle of the dart board is called the bull or bullseye and is worth 50 points.

draughts

    (pronounced *drafts)* checkers

fox hunting

bloodsport described by Oscar Wilde as 'the unspeakable in full pursuit of the uneatable'

SPORT

Glorious Twelfth

12 August, the day the shooting season begins. Traditionally a social occasion for the wealthy and upper classes, people gather by invitation at large country houses – typically in the north of England and in Scotland – and form shooting parties. Hired men called beaters scare the birds and the shooters stand in one spot and bring down as many birds as they can, usually a great number in all.

golf

Britain gave the world golf although, in this case, Scotland gets the credit. St Andrews course in Fife is officially the address of world golf, home to the Royal & Ancient Club which is the recognised authority on the rules of the game. There are golf courses throughout Britain for those who want to participate, and major tournaments (including the British Open) throughout the summer for those who prefer to watch.

lawn bowls

this is a very old game with an outdated reputation for attracting very old players. It's played with balls (called bowls) which are made of wood, Bakelite or hard rubber. The bowl is slightly out of spherical shape and weighted on one side so it will run in a curved course. It has no holes, it's smaller than a bowling ball, and it weighs less. The game is played outdoors on a green by the players rolling bowls at a smaller, target white ball (the jack), trying to get as close to it as possible. There's no penalty for hitting it. It sounds simple but don't be deceived – it's not. Perhaps only those mature in years have the patience to master it.

lawn tennis

tennis. Since tennis first became an established sport in England, when it was played on a grass court, they've used 'tennis' only as a shortened form of lawn tennis. In the sports section of English newspapers, where tennis results from Australia, Germany, France and the US are reported, the column is headed 'lawn tennis' even when games played on clay courts and hard courts are listed.

ninepin bowling
similar to tenpins or the game many other countries simply call 'bowling'

noughts and crosses
tic-tack-toe

Oxford and Cambridge Boat Race
this is a rowing race between teams of eight from the two oldest universities in England and takes place annually in late March or early April. The race dates from 1829 and is billed as the world's longest surviving sporting rivalry. The race distance is 6800m – three times the Olympic distance. The race has never been cancelled due to bad weather despite treacherous conditions which have caused boats to sink in the past. Oxford traditionally had the upper hand but Cambridge dominated the race throughout the 1990s.

pitch
playing field

ride to hounds
ride a horse behind a pack of hounds chasing a fox or a stag

skittles/ninepins
nearly the same as tenpins, or bowling. There's also a table version of this game, called table skittles.

sledge
sled

snooker
a game in the order of pool or billiards, which attracts great interest and good television coverage in Britain (although we're hard pressed to think of a duller TV spectacle).

SPORT

There are 15 red balls and six balls of other colours – yellow, green, brown, blue, pink and black. Each time you pot a red ball you score one point and get the opportunity to pot a colour. The colours are worth more, two points for a yellow ascending to seven points for the black. The red stays in the pocket after it's potted, but the colours are replaced in their original position. Once all the reds are off the table, the colours must be potted in a set order (as above). The table is about four times the size of a pool table. You're snookered when your opponent has left you without a clear shot at the ball you're aiming for.

When a player pots a ball, he starts a break, which is the value of all the balls the player pots consecutively. The maximum break is 147, when the player pots all the reds, a black after each red, and all the colours. During the height of snooker's popularity in Britain in the early 1980s, the first player to make the maximum 147 break on television was Canadian Cliff Thorburn.

training
    exercising; working out; going to the gym

GOVERNMENT & POLITICS

Here are some terms that could be confusing if you're not yet
familiar with British politics.

another place
  the 'other' House of Parliament – either the House of
  Commons or the House of Lords. Only the English could
  have thought this up. When MPs or people from the House
  of Lords say that this topic was discussed or that bill was
  voted on in another place, they're not being vague or
  forgetful. They know exactly where they're talking about –
  where each other do business in Parliament. As if it were
  taboo, the MPs in the House of Commons don't mention
  the House of Lords by name – they call it another place and
  vice versa. It's all very coy and wry. But that's the British for
  you – they love their bit of witty fun.

Chancellor of the Exchequer
  cabinet minister in charge of the exchequer or national
  treasury (not to be confused with the Lord Chancellor,
  more formally called the Lord High Chancellor)

exchequer
  national treasury

Greens
  one of the minor political parties in Britain. This party
  concentrates mainly on environmental issues.

House of Commons
  lower house of Parliament. This is an elected body whose
  members are called Members of Parliament, or MPs. The
  Prime Minister and the Cabinet are from this house. There are
  651 MPs, the Speaker of the House making up the ultimate
  'one' and casting the deciding vote in case of tied votes.

BRITISH SOCIETY

House of Lords

upper house of Parliament. This is an unelected body, whose members are called Lords Spiritual (bishops and archbishops) and Lords Temporal (peers). Until 1958, all peerages were male and hereditary. In 1958, the Lords (as the House of Lords is called) admitted life peers (non-hereditary titles given to both men and women).

Labour Party

left of centre political party, one of the two major parties in British politics and currently the governing party. The Labour party was formed in 1893 in Bradford under the leadership of Keir Hardie, as the party that would defend the rights of workers.

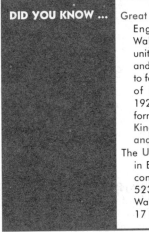

DID YOU KNOW ...

Great Britain is made up of England, Scotland and Wales. England officially united with Wales in 1536, and with Scotland in 1707 to form the United Kingdom of Great Britain. (Since 1921, Northern Ireland has formed part of the United Kingdom of Great Britain and Northern Ireland.)

The UK Parliament is based in England. There are 650 consitutencies, or seats – 523 for England, 38 for Wales, 72 for Scotland and 17 for Northern Ireland.

Law Lord
: also known as a Lord of Appeal, a Law Lord is a member of the House of Lords appointed to take care of the judicial matters of the House

Liberal Democrats
: third strongest political party in Britain

Lord Chancellor
: the highest judicial officer of the United Kingdom and keeper of the Great Seal (the seal used to authenticate important government documents). Presides over the House of Lords, the Chancery Division of the High Court of Justice and the Court of Appeal.

minister
: member of the government with responsibilities in a particular ministry, such as Housing, Trade or Education. In each ministry, the most senior minister is the Secretary of State, who is a member of the Prime Minister's cabinet, followed by Ministers, and then Junior Ministers. Of course, all are accountable to the Prime Minister.

the Opposition
: more formally called Her/His Majesty's Loyal Opposition, this is the principal party opposing the governing party in the British Parliament

Parliament
: the supreme legislature of Great Britain. The British Parliament is universally thought of as 'the Mother of all Parliaments'. It was founded on the English Parliament, formed during the 13th century from the great councils of the Plantagenet kings.

The origin of the word goes back even earlier. William the Conqueror is said in the Chronicle to have had 'very deep speech' with his Witan, and 'deep speech' was, in the Conqueror's French language, *parlement*. Simon de Montfort's parliament of 1265 and Edward I's Model Parliament of 1295 were the first two actual parliaments, since those who assembled were not only the nobles, but commoners as well.

In the 14th century the English Parliament assumed the right to make laws and control taxation. The division into Lords and Commons became permanent under Edward III, who reigned from 1327 to 1377. The Long Parliament, sitting from 1640 to 1653, opposed Charles I in England's Civil War, and after Charles was beheaded in 1649, Parliament ruled England under a written republican constitution. In 1660 the king was restored to the throne in the person of Charles II, but the problem of which powers should be the monarch's and which should be Parliament's still remained. In this period, the beginnings of the party division into Whigs and Tories occurred.

During the 18th century, the Cabinet and the office of Prime Minister developed. Throughout the 19th century – beginning with the Reform Act of 1832 and ending with the Reform Act of 1884 – the electorate was widened to the point of complete manhood suffrage, meaning that virtually all men could stand for election, whether or not they owned property or possessed a designated amount of wealth. The Whig Party also became the Liberals in the 19th century.

During the 20th century, the newly formed Labour Party returned its first members to Parliament, women obtained the right to stand for election, and in 1911, the Parliament Act limited the power of the House of Lords, giving legislative supremacy to the Commons.

Parliament's term is five years, but a government may hold a general election earlier if it chooses.

quango

an acronym for 'quasi-autonomous non-governmental organisation'. This is a semi-public administrative body, outside the Civil Service but receiving financial support from the government. Its senior members are appointed by the government. These are controversial organisations which were set up under the Tory government, resulting in bitter complaint that Britain has too much specially appointed, non-elected government.

reshuffle

interchange of posts of Government ministers which occurs every year or so. In a reshuffle, ministers may lose their post entirely or may simply move to a different post, say from Agriculture Secretary to Education Secretary.

Secretary of State

senior minister who heads a government department such as Education or Health

shadow cabinet

the body of members of the Opposition who would be Cabinet ministers if that party became the Government

shadow ministers

Members of Parliament from the Opposition on the Shadow Cabinet

the silly season

the late-summer period when Parliament and the Law Courts aren't sitting. Because it's a slow news time, news-papers publish trivial items and endless speculation about policies the political parties are developing for the autumn.

BRITISH SOCIETY

surgery
> session in which an MP opens his or her office to constituents to listen to their troubles and gripes. It has nothing whatever to do with medical operations.

Tories
> the Conservatives, a right of centre political party which is one of the two major parties in British politics. The Tories were first dubbed the 'Conservatives' by Robert Peel in his 1834 Tamworth Manifesto, when he called the opposing party (the Whigs) the party of destruction, and said the Tories would preserve everything good in the nation's institutions and not oppose making changes for the better where needed.

NATIONAL IDENTITY

Generally, the peoples of Scotland and Wales have retained a strong sense of national identity. Scotland has a separate Church and its own systems of law, banking and education, and Wales has its own National Assembly.

Great Britain and England refer to different political entities – the terms aren't interchangeable and to say 'England' when you mean Britain could cause offence.

Lonely Planet

EDUCATION

Every country has its own education system with its variations and complexities. This is just a brief explanation of the basic components of the system in England, which is uniform throughout the country. The system is similar in Wales, but Scotland has its own education system.

A levels (Advanced levels)
    examinations which pupils aspiring to go to university take
    at age 18 as entrance requirements or qualifications

college institute of learning
    a college may be part of a university, like one of the colleges
    of Oxford or Cambridge, or it can be a two- or three-year
    school that students attend after the fifth form. For instance,
    a 'sixth form college' is where students do their sixth form
    study in preparation for their A levels. A vocational col-
    lege is where a student goes to learn a trade. The word is
    used so loosely that it's even sometimes applied to primary
    schools. There are both private and government-funded
    colleges. In England, the word college is *not* used inter-
    changeably with the word university.

comprehensive school
    general secondary school that's publicly funded and requires
    no special testing to enter

form
    grade or level of progression in school. The first form is
    roughly sixth grade, the second form is roughly seventh
    grade, and so on. The following list shows all the forms,
    prefaced with primary school (infant school or grade
    school):

ages 5–11	primary school
age 12	first form
age 13	second form
age 14	third form
age 15	fourth form
age 16	fifth form
ages 17 and 18	sixth form

grammar school

> special secondary school, publicly funded but one that pupils
> must test into by scoring higher than average marks on the
> 11-plus exam (taken at age 11)

GCSEs

> an acronym for General Certificate of Secondary
> Education and the current name for the tests which have
> replaced O levels, these are examinations 16-year-olds
> take to show at what standard they passed their secondary
> education. Mandatory education finishes at age 16 in
> England. GCSE results are shown to employers, or for
> entrance into vocational schools, colleges or sixth-form
> colleges. All 16-year-olds take GCSEs whether they're
> going on to take their A levels or not.

O levels (Ordinary levels)
> see GCSEs

Oxbridge

> portmanteau word for Oxford and Cambridge when
> speaking of the two universities together. When a student
> goes to Oxford or Cambridge, the student is said to be
> going up.

Please, thank you and sorry. You can't use any of
these words often enough. Sorry has some special
uses. A true Englishman, if you step on his foot, will
say 'I'm so sorry' before you have time to apologise,
thus exposing your bad manners and lack of breeding.

S. Burgen

public school
  a bit of a contradiction in terms, this is *not* a publicly funded
  school, nor is it open to the general public. It's a private or
  independent school, an elite institution of learning which is
  costly by anyone's standards. Eton, Rugby, Harrow and
  Winchester are familiar examples. Many pupils who go
  through a public school go on to Oxford or Cambridge –
  in fact, King Henry VI, having personally founded the
  public school Eton in 1440, a year later founded King's
  College, Cambridge, to receive its scholars.

reader
  university lecturer of the highest academic ranking, below
  that of professor, in both teaching and research

revise
  study for an exam; review. When British students talk about
  revising they don't mean rewriting a paper, but will say
  things like, 'I have to stay home tonight and revise for my
  biology exam'.

school leaver
  someone who's leaving high school or secondary school
  permanently.
      In Britain, students don't all finish secondary school at
  the same stage. Students who don't plan to go on to university study stop high school at age 16. Students who hope to
  go to a university attend high school until they're 18. The
  last two years of secondary school are called the sixth form.

supply teacher
  substitute teacher

swot
  to study intensively for an examination. A person who does
  this on a regular basis is called a swot.

tuition
> teaching; private or class lessons; tutoring. In Britain, tuition doesn't generally mean the money you have to pay to go to a university. In the past, students haven't been charged fees for attending university, although this is being phased out.

university lecturer
> person who teaches at a university. In Britain, as elsewhere in Europe, a professor is a rare species. People who get their PhDs and are hired by a university aren't automatically designated 'professor'. Professorships are positions that open up, traditionally one to a department, and are occupied by people who retain the position until they move to a more coveted post in another university, retire, or pass into the world beyond. The main difference between a lecturer and a professor is that professors not only teach and research, but take on the administration of a department as well.

TITLES & FORMS OF ADDRESS

In case you find yourself having tea with the Queen or hob-nobbing with nobility, you'll have to know how to address people. In direct conversation, the following people are addressed in the following manner:

Your Majesty
> the king or queen

Your Royal Highness
> the monarch's spouse, children, sisters and brothers

Your Highness
> the monarch's nephews, nieces and cousins

Your Grace
> a duke/duchess; an archbishop of the Anglican Church

Peers

This is the nobility of England. Those below the rank of duke, duchess or archbishop of the Anglican church are all addressed as Lord or Lady. Female peers are called by their first name (Lady Jane, Lady Mary) while male peers are called by their family name (Lord Hattersley, Lord Chalfont). The peers' titles in order of their ranking are:

> Duke, Duchess
>
> Marquis (also spelled Marquess)/Marchioness
>
> Earl/Countess
>
> Viscount/Viscountess
>
> Baron/Baroness

Baronets and knights and their spouses aren't peers. They're called Sir and Lady. Members of Her Majesty's Privy Council and Cabinet Ministers are called Right Honourable.

The practice, in England, of calling a duke, a marquis, an earl or a viscount by the name of the place of their title (they're always the Duke of someplace and the Marquis of someplace and the Earl of someplace or other), rather than the names they were born with, can be confusing for people from countries without nobility.

If you hear someone say, 'Well, Buckingham, how goes it?', you might guess they're using someone's title. But it's not always that easy. In Shakespeare's *Richard III*, you'll see dialogues between Richard and Clarence. You can be forgiven for thinking they're both using first names, but not so. Richard is being called by his first name because he's king, but not Clarence. Clarence is a duchy, and the one being called 'Clarence' is the Duke of Clarence. Actually, his name is George. Before Richard became king, he was the Duke of Gloucester, and he was called

'Gloucester' on those pages, but is called 'Richard' later. So it helps to keep these things in mind when talking to or reading about titled people.

The historical figure called 'King-maker' is an apt example. He was born Richard Neville, but he was also the Earl of Salisbury and called 'Salisbury'. Later, he became the powerful 16th Earl of Warwick, and was then called 'Warwick'. Benjamin Disraeli is another example. If you want to read his works and look in the stacks under the D's you may not find him, as he's often shelved in the B section. He was called 'Beaconsfield' since Queen Victoria made him Earl of Beaconsfield.

AMERICAN – BRITISH

SPELLING
This section will make you aware of the sorts of differences that occur between British and American spellings.

Suffixes
-tre
Some words ending in -tre in Britain end in '-ter' in the US.

centre
litre
metre
theatre

-our
Many British English words ending in -our end in '-or' in the US.

colour
endeavour
honour
labour
neighbour
savour

-ise
US words ending in '-ize' like 'apologize' sometimes end in -ise in Britain, although there is a trend toward using '-ize'.

aggrandise
finalise
pluralise
terrorise

Words

aluminium

the British both spell and pronounce this differently from the way Americans do. The US version has four syllables with the stress on the second syllable (*a-lu-min-um*). The British say it in five syllables, with the stress on the third syllable (*a-lu-mi-ni-um*).

cheque

is the British English spelling for 'check'

connexion

is how 'connection' has been traditionally spelled in Britain, but it is now giving over to the American spelling

defence

is the British English spelling for 'defense'

draught

has gone out of usage in the US – Americans spell it 'draft'. Nevertheless, both draught and draft are pronounced *draft*. The general meaning is 'to pull or to draw'. So we get words and meanings in Britain like the air current in a room ('It's draughty in here'), the drawing of liquid from a receptacle (such as draught beer), a drink or swallow of something (a draught of water), draught horse (a horse that pulls things), and draughtsman or draughtswoman (a man or woman who draws a pencil across a page).

The British also have a few words that they actually do spell 'draft' as Americans do. They draft someone into the army. They write a draft at the bank to take out money, and they write a first draft of a letter, essay or report.

furore

(pronounced *fyur-or-ee* in three syllables with the last syllable pronounced like the last syllable in 'recipe'). This is the preferred spelling and pronunciation of the word in Britain. The American 'furor' (pronounced *fyur-or* in two syllables) is Britain's second preference.

gaol

The words gaol and Geoffrey look exotic, but they're just plain old 'jail' and 'Jeffrey' and are pronounced the same. The spellings are hold-overs from the period of about three and a half centuries following the invasion of England by the Norman French (1066) when French was the written and spoken language in England for all but the lower classes. Old French for 'jail' is *gaole* and for 'Jeffrey' is *Geoffroy*.

kerb

the British English spelling for 'curb', meaning 'edge of the pavement'. However, the British spell the verb meaning 'to cut back on something' as curb.

programme

spelled like this in Britain, but pronounced as 'program' is in the US

tonne

pronounced the same as 'ton', and means the metric ton (1000kg). The imperial ton, or long ton (1016kg), is also used in Britain.

waggon

may be spelled with two g's in Britain

TERMS & PHRASES

agony aunt

Dear Abby (advice column)

carry on

continue

AMERICAN – BRITISH

a dog's breakfast
popular term in Britain for any strange collection of things, hodge-podge or weird mixture

drink driving
drunk driving

finish up with
end up with

funnily enough
oddly enough. The phrase funnily enough simply doesn't exist in countries like the US and Canada, where 'funny' is used only as an adjective. The British, however, are more versatile and use the word both as an adjective and an adverb.

gone off
spoiled; gone bad; gone rotten

it's your go
it's your turn

the last but one
the second last one

made redundant
dismissed from a job, usually with pay. The phrase made redundant is very familiar in Britain as a way of saying someone lost his or her job because their position became obsolete. They're given a sum of money when they leave, based on their length of service and pay. There are two forms of being made redundant – voluntary redundancy and involuntary redundancy. In both cases, you go.

next door but one
two doors away

past its sell-by date
a popular expression in Britain for anything that's passé or out-of-date. They even use it for a person who has become a

bore or has lost his usefulness (He's past his sell-by date). This, of course, comes from the expiration date marked on food products, which in Britain is called the sell-by date and which the British pay scrupulous attention to and religiously adhere to.

Thursday week
a week from Thursday

to the ...
in Britain, they don't say 'March 1st through August 5th' as they do in some English-speaking countries, meaning 'through to and including' the 5th. The British simply say to the 5th and understand that to mean the 5th is included. They also write their dates differently from the way Americans do – 1/3/68 (the 1st of March, 1968) in Britain is 3/1/68 (March 1st, 1968) in the US. In other words, Britain (and all of Europe) has first the day, then the month, then the year. Keep that in mind when you make reservations or you can get your plans really fouled up.

the washing up
the dirty dishes

wouldn't touch it with a bargepole
wouldn't touch it with a ten-foot pole

Differences in Phrasing

Among English-speaking countries, some differences in phrasing occur because one word – usually a preposition – is different.

about
around. Some British English speakers may say 'I looked about me' as an alternative to 'I looked around me'.

or, alternatively
or else. It's common to say 'You can do this, or, alternatively, you can do that' (you can do this, or else you can do that).

AMERICAN – BRITISH

ask after someone
  ask about someone

down to
  be responsible for (It's a good plan, but it's down to the
  teachers to make it work.)

on heat
  in heat (The cat's on heat.)

on the cards
  in the cards

to take a decision
  in Britain, you can either take a decision, perhaps from a
  pile of them lying around, or make a decision, seemingly
  creating it from scratch

FUNNILY ENOUGH

The phrase funnily enough, meaning 'oddly
enough' simply doesn't exist in some countries. The
British are versatile, using funny both as an adjective and an adverb.

BRITISH WORDS
There are some very common words in Britain which aren't used
in the US, and it'll save you inevitable frustration to know the
main ones.

acclimatised
  acclimated

ante-natal
  pre-natal (as in the care of pregnant women)

anti-clockwise
counter-clockwise

bandage
elastic bandage (strip of material for binding up a wound or for use as a blindfold). The little stick-on thing called a 'bandage' or 'Band-Aid' in the US is called a plaster in Britain.

bank holiday
legal holiday

bit
part. The British say 'which bit would you like?' (which part would you like?) or 'it fell to bits' (it fell apart) or 'gather up all these bits' (gather up all these parts). They even speak of body parts as bits, as in 'the doctor examined all my bits'.

brasses
inscribed monumental or sepulchral tablets of brass, marking graves in churches or cemeteries

brilliant
great/terrific/awesome

budgie/budgerigar
a type of small parrot

building society
savings and loan bank. American savings and loan associations were begun in 1831, and were modelled after the British building societies.

cannabis
marijuana. The British normally use the word cannabis rather than 'marijuana'. If there's any difference between the two, it's that cannabis is the Indian hemp, and marijuana is the Indian hemp especially prepared for smoking.

cases
suitcases

chap
   man

chat show
   talk show

clever
   intelligent/smart. This word is used differently in Britain
   from the way it is in the US. For instance, the British speak
   of a clever student, meaning simply a good student or an
   intelligent student, not one who figured out how to get a
   string of A's without opening a book. 'Clever' in the US
   means something in the order of shrewd, ingenious, sly, or
   cunning. In Britain it simply means bright or intelligent.

cling film
   transparent food wrap

clothes-peg/peg
   clothes-pin

cockerel/cock
   rooster

cotton wool
   cotton ball

CHEQUE

cheque is the British
English spelling for
'check'

cuddle
   hug. The British tend to say, 'give me a cuddle' rather than
   'give me a hug'.

cutlery
   silverware; flatware; eating utensils

FALL

'Fall' isn't a season in Britain – they say autumn.

decorate

to paint or wallpaper. The word decorate in Britain is like the word 'redecorate' in the US, but only means painting the walls or repapering – not getting new drapes or carpeting or furniture.

deputise

to function as a substitute or a fill-in. If a British person says to you, 'I'm going to deputise this afternoon' don't say, 'Deputise who?'. They aren't going to pin a tin star on anyone, or form a posse – they're merely going to take over someone else's duties for the day.

direct action

a protest in the form of a march, sit-in or strike

dishcloth

dishrag

drawing pins

thumb tacks

dumb

mute (not stupid)

fancy

imagine; individual taste; liking. Some uses are: 'Fancy that!' (Imagine that!) or 'He fancies himself as quite a lover' (He thinks he's quite a lover) or 'Do you fancy a walk on the beach' (Would you like a walk on the beach?) or 'Nick fancies Sue' (Nick likes Sue).

fête

(pronounced *fate*) to honour; to celebrate; fair held to raise money for charity. Though fête is occasionally used in the US, you don't hear it nearly as much as in Britain. (He's being fêted at the banquet on Saturday night; Are you going to the church fête next week?)

AMERICAN – BRITISH

first/second floor

this ambiguity in terms always provides loads of fun for tourists on the wrong end of it. Throughout Europe, they start counting floors with the first one above ground level. For that reason, all the floors in a building are labelled one number lower than an American would expect. In Britain, be prepared to climb a flight of steps to arrive at the 1st floor. The 3rd floor, to you, will unfortunately be only the 2nd floor, and the 4th floor will, sadly, be only the 3rd.

flannel

washcloth

fortnight

two weeks

fringe

bangs

fusty

musty

PROGRAMME

programme is spelled like this in Britain, but pronounced as 'program' is in the US

a go

a turn/try (Do you want to have a go?)

to grill

to broil; to cook or sear under electric coils or gas flame. In the US, the grill is the cooker in the backyard. In Britain, the grill is the broiler in the oven. Some British appliances have the broiler (the grill) installed in a raised position above the stove top, under a hood. When the British say they're going to grill a piece of meat, they mean they're going to broil it in the oven.

grip

bobby pin

half-four/half-five

four-thirty/five-thirty (in telling the time)

hire
> rent. In Britain, you can hire a car or a bike or a tuxedo, as well as rent one.

holiday
> vacation. In speaking of a trip or time off from work, the British say holiday. (They've gone on holiday; I don't have to go in to the office this week – I'm on holiday.)

homely
> domestic (not plain-looking)

jolly
> very (That's jolly decent of you.)

jug
> pitcher

kettle
> tea kettle. Apart from fish kettle, the British don't use the word kettle to mean merely a pot or pan – it specifically means a tea kettle.

ladybird
> ladybug

layabout
> malingerer. Person who doesn't attempt to find work.

(dog) lead
> (dog) leash

life assurance
> life insurance. In Britain, a policy on your house or car is 'insurance' as in the US. But a policy on your life is called life assurance.

lift
> elevator

lot
> group or bunch of people; faction (You don't want to fall in with that lot.)

mad
> insane (not angry)

midges
> gnats; tiny mosquitoes found in Scotland

Mothering Sunday
> Mother's Day. The British version of this day is based on the church calendar, and is on the fourth Sunday in Lent

muck(y)
> dirt(y). In the US, 'muck' is sludge – something moist and dark and decomposing, a swampy, pitchy substance one wouldn't be thrilled about touching. In Britain, however, it isn't nearly so odious – it's just another word for dirt of any sort, and where Americans would say a thing is dirty, the British would be just as likely say it's mucky.

musical box
> music box

nail varnish
> nail polish

nan
> granny/grandma

nets
> sheers (the filmy curtains that go between the heavier curtains and the window)

notice board
> bulletin board

Pancake Day
Shrove Tuesday, the day before the beginning of Lent. Traditionally, Pancake Day was a way for people to use up their eggs, milk and flour before the fast. Now, for many people, it's a pretty good excuse to stuff yourself with pancakes sprinkled with sugar and lemon juice, jam or syrup. Pancake Day Races, for which contestants are armed with pancakes and frying pans, are held throughout Britain.

persons
people. The British use persons as the plural for 'person' more freely than in the US.

plaster
Band-Aid (small adhesive and gauze strip or patch to cover a cut or small wound)

THE CITY & WESTMINSTER

The City is the 'square mile' of Inner London on the north bank of the Thames. When people talk about the City, they're usually referring to the commercial circles and business district of this area.

Westminster, a city in itself, adjoins London to the west. The term Westminster also refers to Parliament. Some of London's better known landmarks are in the city of Westminster, including Trafalgar Square, the National Gallery, Leicester Square, the West End theatre district, Covent Garden, Victoria Station, Harrod's department store, Hyde Park, Piccadilly Circus, Soho, the British Museum, Bloomsbury and Scotland Yard.

AMERICAN – BRITISH

PMT (pre-menstrual tension)
PMS (pre-menstrual syndrome)

post
    mail

post/letter/pillar box
    mail box

punters
    the general purchasing public

purse
    billfold/changepurse. What's commonly called a 'purse' in
    the US is called a handbag in Britain.

remit
    (pronounced with the stress on the first syllable, *re-mit*) item
    remitted for consideration; a committee's scope, directives,
    or terms of reference when examining a question or carrying
    out a commission (We can't do any hiring or firing – it's not
    within our remit.)

roll up
    roll-your-own cigarette

row
    (pronounced like *how*) quarrel/argue. Row is used much
    more commonly in Britain than it is in the US, both as a
    noun and as a verb. (They had a row; They've been rowing
    about it.) But in Britain it's used even for mere disagree-
    ments, whereas Americans wouldn't use it unless there really
    was some furious, noisy confrontation.

rubber
    eraser. If your British lover tells you he's looking for his
    rubber, don't get excited – he just needs to erase something.

AMERICAN – BRITISH

sacked
  fired

sanitary towels/pads
  sanitary napkins

scupper
  overcome; surprise and massacre. This is a military term which
  has crept into everyday British speech. So you might scupper
  someone's plans, or scupper the scheme they've set in train.

seaside
  in England, when people plan a holiday, they often go to
  one of the many seaside resorts that are found up and down
  the coastline. Hence they say they're going to the seaside
  rather than to the 'lake' or the 'ocean'.

sellotape
  transparent adhesive tape; sticky tape

serviette
  napkin, normally a paper one

be sick
  vomit. Americans 'throw up' while the English are sick. And
  the result of the regurgitation is also called sick, as in 'Theresa
  had to scrub the carpet because there was sick all over it'.

skip
  dumpster

skive
  shirk or evade a duty; slink away. This colloquial word is
  usually used with off. (This isn't a meeting where you can
  just stand at the back of the room and skive off – you have
  to make your opinion known.)

smart
  fashionable/chic

smellies
scented toiletries such as bubble bath and soap

sorry?
'What did you say?' Sorry is sometimes the hardest word, but not in Britain, where you hear it all the time. When people don't catch what you say the first time, instead of saying, 'Pardon?' or 'Come again?' they'll say Sorry?. They also use it if they simply don't get your point. In addition, they use it for 'excuse me' – if they bump into someone, they'll normally say Sorry rather than 'Pardon me' or 'Excuse me'.

spanner
wrench

stick
cane; walking stick

TO THE ...

to the ... in Britain, they don't say 'March 1st through August 5th' as they do in some English-speaking countries, meaning 'through to and including' the 5th. The British simply say to the 5th and understand that to mean the 5th is included. They also write their dates differently from the way Americans do – 1/3/68 (the 1st of March, 1968) in Britain is 3/1/68 (March 1st, 1968) in the US. In other words, Britain (and all of Europe) has first the day, then the month, then the year. Keep that in mind when you make reservations or you can get your plans really fouled up.

stone

  unit of measurement, equivalent to 6.3 kg (14 pounds). If
  you weigh 60kg (132 pounds), for instance, your weight in
  Britain would be 9 stone 6 pounds.

stop

  stay (I packed a bag and stopped overnight at Joan's; Don't
  stop in the sun too long.)

superannuated

  retired

suss

  investigate; find out

sussed

  well informed; in the know

tap

  spigot/faucet

tearaway

  juvenile delinquent; wild teenager; hooligan

terry towelling

  terry cloth (the cotton fabric of uncut loops)

tip

  dump; messy or untidy place. A parent might say to a messy
  teenager, 'This room's a tip', meaning it looks like a dump.
  In some public places there are signs that read 'No tipping' –
  and they don't mean money.

toilet

  in Britain, they don't use the euphemism 'bathroom' for
  toilet as Americans do. If someone's using the toilet, they
  say so instead of saying they're 'going to the bathroom',
  seemingly always on the way, never getting there. Of course,
  they don't mean they're in the very toilet, they mean they're

in the 'toilet room'. Advertisers likewise come right out and sell you **toilet tissue**, not 'bathroom tissue'.

The word lavatory is pretty dated and you rarely hear it anymore. The British slang term for the 'john' or the 'can' is the loo. There's also the W.C. (water closet). Although used throughout Europe, it's not commonly used in Britain. As to the action, while Americans speak of having to 'pee', the British are more likely to say they have to have a wee.

torch

flashlight

treble

the word treble is commonly used in giving numbers in Britain. You might be given the number 41666 as 'four one treble six'.

undertaking

understanding/promise/assurance (They gave us the undertaking that they'd do it free of charge.)

to value

to appraise. In the US, if you want to sell your house or get a second mortgage, you get your house 'appraised'. In Britain, you get it valued.

venue

location; site; place of meeting. In the US, the word 'venue' is used almost exclusively in the field of law, designating where a trial or hearing will take place. In Britain, however, it's used in daily conversation. (We've changed the venue for departure tomorrow morning – we'll meet in the car park instead of at the hotel.)

AMERICAN – BRITISH

the washing-up
dirty dishes

washing-up liquid
dishwashing liquid

wind
where in the US people have 'gas', in Britain they have wind.
Colicky babies, for instance, have trapped wind. And while
Americans may occasionally 'let one go', the British break
wind or as the slang goes, they trump. A polite friend might
warn, 'sorry, I just trumped'.

wireless
household radio

wool
yarn. Yarn is always called wool, even if it's made from
purely cotton or acrylic materials.

Ambiguous Terms

Some ambiguous terms could cause confusion or embarrassment.
Many of these words have the same meaning in Britain as they do
in the US. But each word also has an alternative meaning that
isn't normally used in the US.

chemist
pharmacist (not just a person who works in a chemistry lab)

consultant
specialist – a medical doctor such as a cardiologist,
paediatrician or gynaecologist

dear
expensive or costly

diary
:   appointment book

fanny
:   may mean buttocks in the US but in Britain a fanny is a vagina

flog
:   to sell or push goods or an idea, usually of a shoddy or questionable nature

surgery
:   GP's office

ABBREVIATIONS & ACRONYMS

AA	stands for both Alcoholics Anonymous and Automobile Association
BABA	Book a Bed Ahead Scheme
B&B	Bed and Breakfast
BBC	British Broadcasting Corporation (radio and television)
BSE	mad cow disease (bovine spongiform encephalopathy). Fatal cattle disease which can be transferred to humans through ingesting infected meat. The human version of the disease is called CJD (Creutzfeldt-Jakob Disease).
BT	British Telecom (Britain's chief telephone system, now privatised)
DI	Detective Inspector
DIY	Do It Yourself. Hardware stores are called DIYs and the abbreviation is used in conversation as well (Where's Brian? – He's at home doing DIY.)
DTI	Department of Trade and Industry
EH	English Heritage
G and T	gin and tonic
MP	Member of Parliament
NHS	National Health Service
NT	National Trust
P	pence

PLC	Public Limited Company
RSPCA	Royal Society for the Prevention of Cruelty to Animals
TIC	Tourist Information Centres
UK	United Kingdom, which includes England, Wales, Scotland and, since 1922, Northern Ireland
VAT	Value Added Tax (sales tax)
WC	water closet (international term for 'toilet')

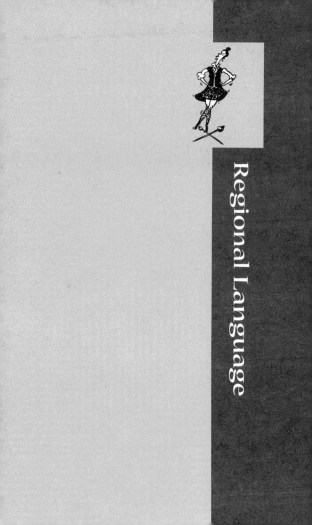

Regional Language

ACCENTS & DIALECTS

Baggings, bait, beaver, bite, biting-on, clocking, crib, crust, dew-bit, docky, dowen, drum-up, forenoon-drinking, jower, lowance, minning-on, nammet, nammick, nummet, nunch(eon), progger, snap, snapping, tenner, tenses, tommy.

Believe it or not, these expressions all mean the same thing – a snack – and they are, or until recently were, all used in various parts of England. This is a country only fractionally larger than the US state of Pennsylvania or New Zealand's North Island, and so for its size the breadth and variety of accents and dialects in use here is remarkable. There's some truth in the observation that an inhabitant of a remoter part of Northumberland speaks almost a different language from someone from rural Cornwall, and yet, these two counties are at most a mere 560 km (350 miles) apart. Despite its pocket-handkerchief dimensions, it's astonishing how linguistically diverse England is, and the traveller should be warned that even if he or she is a native speaker of English, communication can sometimes be quite difficult when trying to hold a conversation with someone who speaks an unfamiliar dialect. This is particularly true in areas that tourists visit less frequently.

Add to England the other constituent countries of Britain – Scotland and Wales – and the situation is yet more complicated. The latter countries are sometimes called the 'Celtic Fringe' and, in both, Celtic languages are still spoken (see pages 199 and 212). The Celtic languages Scottish Gaelic and Welsh have heavily influenced the English spoken in the Celtic countries, in terms of accent, vocabulary and intonation. But the story doesn't end there – a glance at the official statistics for the languages of Britain and its surrounding islands reveals no fewer than 14 – yes, 14 – indigenous languages. Apart from English and the Celtic languages mentioned, these include Cornish (a Celtic language of Cornwall which died out in the late 18th century but which has been revived and is now spoken by some as a second language), Manx (a descendant of Scottish Gaelic formerly spoken throughout the Isle of Man but now only kept up by minority interest groups) and Scots (a language which has been spoken in the south and east of Scotland for at least 900 years, closely related to English, and formerly the official language of Scotland).

French is an official language of the Channel Islands, which lie closer to France than to the English coast. Another island language is Norn, a Scots/Scandinavian dialect which was once spoken in the Orkney and Shetland Islands, but which is now more or less extinct. Various English-based creoles (mostly West Indian varieties such as Jamaican Creole) are spoken in many British cities. And let's not forget the large number of people from Asia in Britain, who come mainly from Pakistan, India, and Bangladesh, but also Hong Kong and Singapore – in certain towns and cities around Britain street signs and public notices may be written in languages like Urdu, Hindi or Cantonese. There are a lot of Greek people in Britain, as well as Turks and people from various Arab countries, so don't be surprised if you see shop signs advertising products and services in unfamiliar alphabets. Luckily, virtually everybody speaks English, so don't worry if you feel your skills as a polyglot aren't up to much.

In fact, if you're interested in hearing indigenous British languages other than English being spoken you may not find it easy. These days, you have to go to north and west Wales or the distant corners of northwestern Scotland to hear Welsh or Scottish Gaelic, as these languages are, unfortunately, under serious threat from the spread of English. But even if English does finally obliterate the other indigenous languages of Britain, it doesn't necessarily mean that we only have a bland, uniform linguistic future to look forward to – the beauty of English is that even though it's already amazingly diverse in terms of its traditional accents and dialects, it also borrows freely from other languages and is constantly refreshed by new terminology and slang. English is in a constant state of change, and always will be, despite the purists' ideas about the importance of preserving the language of Shakespeare and Milton, and it is, I hope you'll agree, all the richer for it.

For the rest of this chapter we'll be looking at some of the varieties of English spoken in the various parts of Britain. Starting in the south-east (London), we'll work northwards up the east coast, round the top of Scotland, and down the west side of the country taking in Wales on the way back. It's probably more important that you get an idea of differences in accent (pronunciation) than differences in dialect vocabulary, because most of the time the person you're talking to will know the equivalent in Standard British English to a dialect word you've found confusing. Someone from an area where a donkey is a pronkus, for instance, will almost always know the word 'donkey' as well. It's possible that some elderly people might find translation of this kind more difficult, but it's unlikely to handicap you in any way. You may, however, confuse people if you use an Australian or US term where the meaning of the word in Standard British English is different – say, if you ask for 'chips' when you want (potato) crisps.

Some information on current slang terms is also included, as – just as in the rest of the English-speaking world – new expressions, idioms and vogue terms come into the language as fashions change. You may be surprised to find that many recent American and Australian slang terms are current among young people in Britain – don't forget that TV shows such as *Friends* and *Neighbours* are extremely popular in Britain, and that trendy words are imported in just the same way that new hairstyles, sporting fashions and the latest in music appear in Britain just days after they come out elsewhere.

Let's kick off in Britain's capital and largest city, London.

South-East England

LONDON & THE SOUTH-EAST

The accents of the south-east of England are closest to what most non-British people will think of when English accents are mentioned. But judging by Dick van Dyke's attempt to sound like a cheery Cockney 'chimbleysweep' in the film *Mary Poppins*, there are some pretty strange ideas about what British English sounds like among North Americans and Antipodeans. In fact, American film stars who can imitate British accents at all convincingly are a rare breed – even the impressively versatile Robin Williams just can't quite cut the mustard when it comes to a Scots brogue in *Mrs Doubtfire*, for example, while Gwyneth Paltrow's stab at a trendy English accent in *Sliding Doors* tends to set one's teeth on edge. As more and more British actors infiltrate the Hollywood movie machine, however, the need for such linguistic gymnastics is reduced, and so over time audiences around the world will get to hear British accents in their original form. It's also becoming more normal for British bands such as Blur and The Proclaimers to sing in their native accents, rather than using the mid-Atlantic accent that used to be favoured by bands like The Beatles, The Rolling Stones and Led Zeppelin.

English accents in London come in three principal flavours:

- the working-class variety known as Cockney (see page 65)

- the elevated speech of the middle and upper classes known as Received Pronunciation (sometimes also known as BBC English, the Queen's English, or Oxford English)

- an intermediate form which has come to be known as Estuary English, as it's spoken in the counties around the estuary of the River Thames

Posh English

Received Pronunciation (RP) needs little introduction – it's the 'posh' English you hear constantly in the media. Think Patrick Stewart in *Star Trek: The Next Generation*, Hugh Grant in *Four Weddings and a Funeral* or Emma Thompson in practically anything, and you've got the general idea. The use of RP is not just confined to the southeast of England, but has become widespread all over Britain. In this way RP speakers are difficult to pigeonhole geographically. RP in fact developed for this very reason, as wealthy families in the 18th century became ashamed of their local speech. You'll hear time and again that RP is the 'best', 'clearest' and 'most beautiful' accent of English, but these views are based on prejudice against other accents as much as anything else. Increasingly, young people in the south of England are becoming less and less attracted by RP speech because of its associations with old-fashioned

ACCENTS & DIALECTS

class-based snobbery, and are turning instead to an accent midway between RP and Cockney which has become known as **Estuary English**. This is quite a recent development in British English – linguists generally agree that it's only been around for the last 20 or 25 years.

Estuary English

The popularity of Estuary English is such that British leader Tony Blair – never known to miss a chance to court public support – has used Estuary pronunciations in his speeches. Of course, this is intolerable behaviour as far as the more conservative 'language guardian' types are concerned. These purists believe that if a Prime Minister starts to use glottal stops in 'a better Britain' (pronouncing the t's as in Cockney 'bottle'), the whole country is bound to go to the dogs. Yet in the last century it was considered perfectly acceptable for politicians to use their own regional pronunciations in parliamentary debates – it seems that the 'Golden Age' of proper English in high places was very short-lived, if it was ever a reality. Nonetheless, certain prominent politicians and educationalists of our own time have even gone so far as to link the use of Estuary English to criminality and other anti-social behaviour. This view is patently absurd, of course, but it shows just how deep-seated prejudices about accents and dialects are in Britain. It seems that rationality often goes by the board when language is at issue. The variations in spoken English around Britain are a subject that virtually any British person will be happy to volunteer an opinion on, and the question of whether change in English is a good or bad thing will almost certainly jerk his or her more conservative knee. Try it!

THE MID-NORTH OF ENGLAND: YORKSHIRE

Moving north, we pass through the notorious Watford Gap, through the flatlands of the East Midlands, and on toward Yorkshire, where the intolerance for 'fancy Southern ways' is extended to include the way English is spoken. A big difference between Yorkshire English and London English that you'll notice straight away is the vowels – where in southern English words like put and putt sound different, in Yorkshire they both sound like put. Likewise, Yorkshire's flat a in pass rhymes with gas, rather than with farce. Remember these pronunciations when you're reciting the mantra that is supposed to have made Yorkshire what it is today – 'Where there's muck there's brass' (meaning wherever there's dirt, there's money to be made).

Of course, in a region the size of Yorkshire – which includes the counties of North, West and South Yorkshire – there's bound to be a good deal of variation in speech patterns. There are quite obvious differences between urban and rural Yorkshire accents, for instance. If you're one of the remaining three people on Earth who hasn't seen *The Full Monty*, I can tell you it's set in the city of Sheffield, in South Yorkshire. Although some of the actors aren't actually natives of Sheffield – notably Robert Carlyle – the Sheffield accents in general are pretty well done. The Leeds and Bradford accents are slightly different from that of Sheffield, while people from the hilly Dale country or the coastal areas have their own subtle speech variations which reflect the isolation of smaller towns and villages from one another right up to the present day. Should you visit small places in the North York Moors or the Yorkshire Dales National Park, you may find the locals, especially older ones, difficult to understand.

There's a wealth of dialect vocabulary used in Yorkshire which will probably be a bit obscure to the traveller. Some of the more common expressions found in Yorkshire are:

Mid-North of England

allus	always
any road (up)	anyway
atta	are you (from 'art thou')
aye	yes
bap	bread roll
beck	a small stream
bonny	fat/plump (Compare this with bonny/bonnie in the North-East of England and in Scotland, where it means pretty, attractive. Avoid saying, 'Oh, you look so bonny in that dress!' when in Yorkshire.)
breadcake	see bap
butty	sandwich
cack-handed	left-handed
chab/chabby/chavvy	child/baby
coursey	pavement/sidewalk
daft	stupid
dale	a valley
gen	gave
	(pronounced with a hard 'g' as in 'get')
gid	see gen
give backword	let down; go back on one's word I were going to meet him at station but he gen backword.
give over; gie owa	stop it; be quiet
gob	mouth
hacky	dirty

happen	maybe
	Happen it is.
ignorant	rude
lake	play
	Yon lad were lakin' in t'ginnel –
	That boy was playing in the alleyway.
lass	girl/woman
loppy	dirty
lugs	ears
manky	dirty
mard-arse	soft/sissy/babyish (see also
	Lancashire mardy on page 210)
neb	nose
nebbin/nebby	nosy
nesh	cold; soft
	You great nesh wazzock!
nowt	nothing
owt	something/anything
parky	cold
	It's a bit parky outside.
right	very
	It's right cold today.
sheggy-handed	see cack-handed
siling down	raining heavily
sithee	see you (goodbye);
	Do you understand?
skinny	tight-fisted/mean

skrike	to cry
sling thee 'ook	get lost (sling your hook)
sock on	fast asleep
wazzock	idiot/buffoon

As in London, h is generally not pronounced at the beginning of a word, so that Yorkshire people will talk about going to 'Arrogate or 'Ebden Bridge. You'll hear Yorkshire folk dropping the word the quite a lot too. Occasionally it's replaced by a short t sound, so that the expression 'I put the baby in the car' might sound like *Ah put babby int car*. Little and bottle are pronounced *lickle* and *bockle* in parts of the county (this is by no means unique to Yorkshire, however), and water may rhyme with 'batter'.

The affectionate term love is used more generally in places like Leeds than it is elsewhere. Don't get the wrong idea if you ask a Yorkshireman the time and he responds, 'Half twelve, love', especially if you're male – it's like pal, mate, or bud(dy) elsewhere. Duck is used in a similar way, but more usually toward women.

The Yorkshire habit of using thee and thou (usually pronounced *tha* or *ta*) can be found elsewhere in northern England, although younger people tend to avoid them as old-fashioned. In other English-speaking countries thee and thou might seem quaintly biblical or wholesome in a Quakery kind of way, but it's simply a relic of earlier forms of English in which the modern multi-purpose you had not yet become the norm.

A word of warning – watch out for Yorkshire while. It doesn't just mean 'while', it can also mean 'until', so shopkeepers will tell you they're open 'nine while five', for example. The tale of the Yorkshireman who came to a level crossing (a crossing over train tracks) and was run down by a train after obeying the sign 'Do not attempt to cross the line while the lights are red' may be a tall story, but it's a good way of remembering this important distinction!

ACCENTS & DIALECTS

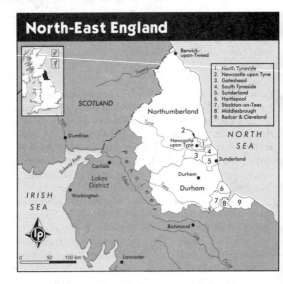

North-East England

Berwick-upon-Tweed

1. North Tyneside
2. Newcastle upon Tyne
3. Gateshead
4. South Tyneside
5. Sunderland
6. Hartlepool
7. Stockton-on-Tees
8. Middlesbrough
9. Redcar & Cleveland

SCOTLAND

Northumberland

NORTH SEA

Dumfries

Newcastle upon Tyne

Carlisle

Lakes District

Sunderland

Durham

Durham

Workington

IRISH SEA

Richmond

Lancaster

0   50   100 km

ACCENTS & DIALECTS

THE NORTH-EAST OF ENGLAND

Travelling north from Yorkshire across the River Tees into County Durham and Northumberland, we reach the north-eastern corner of England. We're now into the land of the Geordies and the Makems – the dialects of the cities of Newcastle and Sunderland are in particular said to be among the most difficult to understand of any English accents.

Newcastle upon Tyne is the biggest city in the far north of England. It's often said that the Geordies (inhabitants of Newcastle) sound more like Scots than they do English people, but this is probably because the city is very close to the border and has always attracted Scots immigrants. Charles Jennings, who says that Geordie 'sounds like ordinary English spoken backwards', tells the story in his book *Up North: Travels Beyond the Watford Gap* of a war veteran he met who insisted that when the Eighth Army was campaigning in North Africa, the Geordie regiments didn't have to use the same code words or radio security as other units. As they were unintelligible to most other native English speakers, the reasoning went, the Germans wouldn't have a hope. Whether this tale is true or not, it's plausible. Having lived for several years in Newcastle I can recall several occasions on which friends from overseas didn't actually realise that local people they heard talking on buses, for example, were speaking English rather than Russian, say, or Danish – though oddly enough, Danish visitors to Newcastle often seem to have an easier time understanding Geordie than some native speakers of English, perhaps because the strong Scandinavian influence in Tyneside has persisted since the days of the Vikings. Anyone coming from another English-speaking country who reckons that all English accents are a pushover (Aw, come on, everyone knows that English blokes talk either like John Cleese or John Lennon, and I can deal with both of those accents!) are in for a surprise here.

Not wanting to frighten anyone further, however, it should be said that people in the north-east are generally very friendly and accommodating, so that if you're obviously struggling to understand someone who comes up to you and says, 'How pet, gannin' doon toon wi' wuh?', he or she will probably try to make life a bit easier for you by translating this into something more recognisable (like 'Hello mate, do you want to go into town with us?').

aal reet?	how are you?
bairn	child/baby
bobbydazzler	smart/attractive
	Ee, that new gansey is a right bobbydazzler.

canny	all-purpose term of approval He's a canny snooker player like.
Champion!	Great!/Terrific!
chin	break Sorry mam, I chinned a plate.
clarts	mud Me clobber's aal clarty – My clothes are all dirty.
div	do (negative divvent) Divvent dee that! Don't do that!
gadgie	an old man, or sometimes an old woman
gan	go Let's gan to the pub.
gansey/ganzie	woolly jumper (after Guernsey, the Channel Island)
geet	very Wor lass is geet bonny – My wife's very pretty.
Geordie	inhabitant of Newcastle upon Tyne (diminutive of George – said by some to be a reference to 'Mad' King George III, and by extension any unpredictable or undesirable person)
glair/glaur	mud
glaky	slow-witted
hadaway	go away; get lost. Also expression of disbelief (see howay/haway).
hinny	term of endearment, like 'honey'

howay/haway	expression of disbelief
	You just swam across the Tyne?
	Howay man, ah divvent believe that like!
	Also can be a term of encouragement
	Haway the Magpies! (the Magpies is the
	nickname for Newcastle United Football
	Club, from their black-and-white stripes)
hoy	to throw
	Hoy it oot the winda! –
	Throw it out of the window!
hyem	home
Makem	rhymes with *pack 'em*. Inhabitant of
	Sunderland. (Said to originate from the
	shipbuilding industry's makem and takem
	– make the ships and take them down
	the river.)
man	can be used of men, women and even small
	children
	Put aal your toys away man Darren.
marrer	(work)mate
mortal	drunk
nettie	toilet
pallatic	drunk
pickle	a small quantity
	Gi's a pickle mair – Give me a bit more.
Pitmatic	special dialect used by coalminers
poke	bag
scutty	scruffy

ACCENTS & DIALECTS

stottie	large flat loaf of bread; oven-bottom cake
whey aye	of course

The pronunciation of the name Newcastle itself is characteristic – the stress goes on the second syllable rather than the first, and as in Yorkshire English, the a is 'flat', so that Newcastle rhymes with 'hassle' rather than 'parcel'. The other vowels are similarly rearranged so that no and do are *nee* and *dee*, take is *tak*, know is *naa*, stone is *steeyen*, house is *hoose* (note that there's no h-dropping in Newcastle), shirt is *shawt* and cold is *caad*. Storytellers and comedians have long taken advantage of the potential confusions caused by these differences. For example, there's a story about a Geordie with an injured knee who goes to see his doctor. The doctor bandages him up, and asks, 'Now then, do you think you can walk?' Geordie looks at him in amazement, and exclaims, 'Walk? I can hardly waak!' ('Work? I can hardly walk!').

In parts of Northumberland people may be heard to use the 'Northumbrian burr', an 'r' sound just like the one in French or German, produced toward the back of the mouth. So in Northumbrian English, brown sounds like German *braun*, and often the vowel is 'oo', as in Newcastle Broon (Newcastle brown ale, nicknamed 'The Dog' – Geet canny yel like, but divvent get pallatic!) There are many other oddities, but the best thing you can do is to go to the north-east and experience the dialect for yourself.

NORTH OF THE BORDER: SCOTLAND

Many people, including a good number of English people, tend to think of Scotland as though it were just another region of England. It isn't, of course, and never has been – Scotland has its own history, culture and languages – and it looks as though the Union with England may soon be coming to an end after an uneasy and sometimes bloody 300 years.

At about the same size as Austria or Portugal, Scotland's also bigger than some people realise. But its population is tiny – less than 5 million - and as a result its larger neighbour England has tended to overshadow it in most ways. Because of its sparse population and mountainous terrain, however, the influence of the English language in some areas of Scotland is quite a recent development. For this reason, across most of the Highlands and Islands, which was (and still is, in parts) a Gaelic-speaking area, there's little dialect variation in the spoken English – Highland English is still too young to have 'gone off and done its own thing'. Some people claim that the English of Inverness is the purest, clearest and least adulterated variety of the language, because it hasn't had time to get 'contaminated' by regional dialects of other parts of Britain. Consequently, this section is relevant only to the areas where English has been spoken for a long time – the so-called Central Belt between Glasgow and Edinburgh, the Borders and the east coast up toward Aberdeen. Note that the similarity of English to the indigenous language Scots means that there's been a lot of mixture between the two languages – the relationship is a bit like that between Swedish and Norwegian, or Spanish and Portuguese, where the languages are almost close enough for people to understand one another.

Apart from the influence of the Worldsh Shexiesht Man Sean Connery – real name Thomas, or Big Tam – Edinburgh English is now world-famous because of *Trainspotting* (not set in Glasgow, though some scenes were filmed there). The pronunciation differences between Edinburgh and Glasgow English are fairly

Scotland

minor, except for the giveaway intonation pattern in Glaswegian. It's difficult to represent on paper, but have a listen to Glasgow comedian Billy Connolly and you'll get the gist! The rash of films with Scottish themes has raised the profile of Scots speech a little too – Mel Gibson in *Braveheart* maintained a very commendable, if modern-sounding, Scottish accent as William Wallace, while Ulsterman Liam Neeson just about pulled it off in *Rob Roy* (Jessica Lange ... well, she had a go, to put it diplomatically – her accent 'occasionally takes the high road while she takes the low', to quote the film critic Jim Byerley).

Any difficulties you may have if you go to the cities of central Scotland are as nothing compared to those associated with the 'Doric' dialect of Scots spoken in and around the city of Aberdeen. The Scandinavian influence is obvious in the Granite City – more than once I've been fooled into thinking that Aberdonians were speaking Norwegian when they were using their vernacular speech. Annie Lennox, formerly of the Eurythmics, is an Aberdonian most people will have heard of, but virtually all traces of the Doric have now been ironed out of her English – certainly, you don't often hear her say Tyaavin awa or Gweed 'I'm fine'/'Good' in answer to the Aberdonian greeting Fit like? 'How are you?', or Hine awa 'far away' to Far d'ye bide? 'Where do you live?'. Aberdonians call bumble bees foggie-bummers and earwigs horny-gollochs, foreigners are fremmit and dubs is mud. To list more, however, would be orra (spare, extraneous, untidy).

The use of the trilled Scottish 'r' (à la Scrooge McDuck and Willy the janitor from *The Simpsons*) is a touch exaggerated – it's actually fairly infrequent in modern Scottish English. But like most American, Canadian or Irish accents, the 'r' in words like car, four, barn and first is fully sounded, rather than dropped as is the case with many accents of England, where paw sounds the same as pour, pore and often poor. Scots home is hame, stone is stane, long is lang, and head and dead are pronounced heed and *deed*. You'll also hear the guttural 'ch' sound used quite a bit by Scots, in words like loch, dreich, or the exclamation Och! It's just like the German 'ch' in *Bach*, *Loch*, or *acht*, or the 'j' of Spanish *mujer*, *Baja*, *Juan*. And as in Newcastle English, Scottish people will say *hoose* for house, *oot* for out and *doon* for down.

In former times Scots had its own semi-standardised spelling system, which includes some unusual conventions – if, for instance, you see a 'z' in Scots names like Menzies, Culzean and Dalziel, it should be pronounced *ng* or *y* – thus, *Mingis*, *Cullain* and *Dayell*. The odd-looking sequence 'quh' as in Urquhart, Farquhar, Colquhoun and Balquhidder was not intended as a *kw* sound. Instead, it sounded like the noise you make when blowing out a candle. So while most people would now say the surnames *Urkert* and *Farker*, the place-name Balquhidder (where you can see the real Rob Roy's grave) is still pronounced *Bal-whidder*, and Colquhoun *Col-hoon*.

There's only enough space here to list a tiny fraction of Scots words that are still used – the Scots National Dictionary runs to ten volumes of several hundreds pages each – but here's a taster of some of the words and phrases you may come across:

ay	yes
aye	always (ay and aye sound the same, like 'eye')
barry	excellent (apparently a Gypsy word)
	That fitba match wis pure barry.
ben	hill or mountain (from Gaelic beinn);
	into
	Come ben the hoose.
blether	drivel/waffle
boggin	disgusting/unpleasant/ugly
bowfin	disgusting/unpleasant/ugly
braw	great/good
burn	stream/brook

cannae	can't
ceilidh	party/dance/get-together (Gaelic for 'meeting', pronounced *kaylie*)
cheg	to steal
chore/chorie	see cheg
clan	family; group of related families (from Gaelic clann meaning 'children')
clanjamfrie/ clamjamfry	a crowd; odds and ends
clarty	dirty/muddy
clingin	disgusting/unpleasant/ugly
clipe	to tell on someone
crabbit	bad tempered; sullen
dead	very/extremely Ah hink the Jam Tarts are dead brilliant! – I think Hearts (Heart of Midlothian Football Club) are great!
dinnae	don't
dinner	lunch
dram	a measure of spirits
dreich	miserable/wet/gloomy (of weather)
forbye	as well; also
gallus	mischievous
gey	very It's gey cauld the day.
glaikit	slow-witted/gauche (see Newcastle glaky)
glen	valley (from Gaelic gleann)
gnash	to hurry C'moan youse, gnash!

gowk	idiot/fool (lit: a cuckoo)
greet	to cry Dinnae greet, it's jist a skelf! – Don't cry, it's only a splinter!
haar	thick, damp mist coming in off the sea
Haud yer whisht!	Be quiet!
haver	to chatter aimlessly or foolishly; to waffle
hen	term of endearment (used toward women). Also doll.
high tea	large meal of sandwiches, cakes and tea eaten in the late afternoon
Jings!	Good heavens! (or words to that effect)
ken	know D'ye ken yon laddie? – Do you know that boy over there?
loch	lake
loon(ie)	boy/lad
loup	to run/jump
lum	a chimney
mingin	disgusting/unpleasant/ugly
mizzle	light rain (lighter than drizzle)
muckle/mickle	big
nip	a measure of spirits
nyaff	idiot
pech	pant/puff (often after climbing a ben)
peelie-wally	(rhymes with 'alley') pale/sickly- looking/weak

quean; queen	girl/woman
radge	(n) slightly deranged person See that radge? (adj) something exciting or out of the ordinary He's totally radge, ken?
rare	great/good
reek	smoke (like German *Rauch* – hence Auld Reekie 'Old Smoky', the nick name for Edinburgh
Sassenach/ Sassunach	an English person (slightly insulting – but actually this can be applied to English-speaking Scots as well – it's from the Gaelic word for 'Saxon')
scaff	tramp; badly-dressed person
scunnered	disgusted/repelled
shan	bad/awful/unkind
shoogle	to shake
Slàinte!	(pronounced *slandge*) Cheers!
stoor	dust
stoorie	hurry; run away
strath	valley (from Gaelic srath)
swally	(alcoholic) drink
tea	evening meal (also the drink)
Teuchter	a Highlander (mocking)
the day	today
the morn	tomorrow The morn's morn – Tomorrow morning.
wouldnae	wouldn't

There are some peculiar grammatical constructions you may hear in Scottish English.

My hair needs washed.
My hair needs washing/a wash.

Eh you're a Hibee.
Confirm that you're a supporter of Hibernian Football Club.

I might could go the morn.
I might be able to go tomorrow.

There it's!
There it is!

That cup's mines.
That cup is mine.

The last example might sound odd, but if you think about it, it's more logical than the Standard British English equivalent, since in Standard English you'd say That cup's his, hers, yours, ours, theirs, and Bob's, but mine, which for some reason has no 's' on the end.

That's me means 'I'm finished', while I'm away means 'I'm leaving now'. A useful feature of Scottish English is the distinction between you (sg) and youse (pl) – it makes things clearer if you can distinguish between Are you coming doon ma bit later on? and Are youse coming doon ... ? when speaking to several people at once. Try pointing this out to the kind of people who write to the BBC demanding subtitles for TV programmes featuring Scottish accents, however, and you won't get far – like Geordie, Glaswegian English is a serious contender in the unintelligibility stakes as far as most of the British are concerned.

We turn back south across the border now to look at dialects of north-western England – those of Cumbria, Lancashire, Manchester and Liverpool.

North-West England

THE NORTH-WEST OF ENGLAND

Stretching from Scotland to the Welsh border along the coast of the Irish Sea, the north-western part of England is characterised by dialects which are very similar to those of Yorkshire, County Durham and Northumberland on the other side of the Pennine Hills. Book and buck sound the same, while the vowel of the words path, grass and fast is short or 'flat' as in Yorkshire. Many of the dialect words used are the same too – a bap is a bread roll, your lug is your ear, and backend is autumn (fall). Nonetheless, get a Lancastrian confused with a someone from Yorkshire and you could be in for trouble – the rivalry between these counties goes back to the War of the Roses and probably long before that.

Beginning with Cumbria, often said to be England's most beautiful county, we see again that remoteness from large cities in combination with rugged terrain has helped to preserve speech forms from much earlier times. The dialectologist Peter Wright has collected a huge number of unusual expressions and pronunciations from the area, introducing his book *Cumbrian Chat: How it is Spoke* by commenting,

> Ah knaw ivverybody dizna leyk it – they say it's nee way o' talkan, nut BBC keynd or owt o' that. But, if it dizna impress thee, there's summat wrang: thoo's a dummleheed, sackless, gawmless, nicked i' t'heed or jiggered. Even leyl lads can speak it.

Cumbrian broadcaster and novelist Melvyn Bragg disagrees, however – in a recent survey of 'leyl lads' at primary schools in Cumbria he found that many of them had never heard the traditional dialect words before, and had no idea what they meant. Such loss of local dialect terminology in Cumbria is, sadly, absolutely typical of modern Britain, just as it is in many other places that speak English. Wright isn't complacent – he laments, for example, the recent extinction of the 1400-year-old Celtic-based number system used for counting livestock in Cumbria. You won't hear yan, tyan, tethera, methera, pimp, sethera, lethera, hovera, dovera and dick through bumfit (15) up to giggot (20) at sheep auctions these days. So if you want to hear the echoes of what English might have sounded like in previous centuries, go to tucked-away hamlets at the heads of remote dales and eavesdrop on locals in shops and pubs. But do it now – another generation or two and it may be too late.

By the way, don't be surprised if someone asks you if you'd like a shag in Cumbria – it's a sandwich!

Just to the south of Cumbria's Lake District we come into Lancashire. Lancashire speech, as mentioned above, is quite similar to Yorkshire English, though in parts of the county the 'r' of words like corn, skirt or farmer is pronounced, as in American English. In broad Lancashire accents, asking may be heard as *axin*, bowls may be *bowels*, water *watter*, wash *wesh*, and wrong *wrang*.

Some of the terms listed below may be found in the cities of Liverpool and Manchester, which were until the 1970s both within the borders of Lancashire.

bally-wart	stomachache
barm/batch	bread roll
beawnt	going to
brid	a child (from 'bird')
camp	to chat
chuck	term of endearment (as in the greeting Eh up chuck)
cob on	annoyed E's getten a cob on – He's annoyed.
collops	lots of
estin	dustbin/trashcan
ey lads ey	reality/basics When it comes to ey lads ey.
fain	glad
fratch	to argue
frimbles	nervous/uncertain
giggle gaggle	passage between houses
ginnel	see giggle gaggle
Gobbinland	Oswaldtwistle (town near Blackburn, gobbin being a kind of slag from open pit mines)
hoo	she

jannock	reasonably good
keawer	sit
Lanky	Lancashire, or inhabitant of that county
lish	agile/fit
lobby gobbler	native of Leigh (lobby comes from lobscouse, a kind of stew – see page 285)
mardy	grumpy/moody
moggy	as elsewhere, a cat – in West Lancashire, a mouse!
moither	annoy
nazzy	bad-tempered
nouse	(rhymes with house) common sense/ intelligence E's got no nouse.
po fagged	exhausted
pownd	stressed A'm pownd t'deeath.
shive	slice of bread
sken	to look
sneck	nose
tara	goodbye
utch	to move
us	our This is us new house.
wick	quick; agile; heaving with Wick wi' mice.

Dust is 'do you?' as in *Dust come frae Darrun?* 'Do you come from Darwen?' and, like in Yorkshire, *thee* and *thou* can still be heard occasionally.

If you can receive the world's longest-running TV soap opera *Coronation Street*, which is set in Manchester, watch a few episodes before you leave – think of it as an immersion course in broad 'Manc'. And should you be in need of clarification at any point, David Hannah has compiled an entire on-line dictionary dedicated solely to what he calls 'Le Patois de Corrie' – yes, it's a bit sad, but this program is a national obsession and is still far and away the most popular show on British television. Alternatively, Jane Leeves does a passable Manc as Daphne Moon in *Frasier*, and she's a good deal easier on the ear than *Coronation Street's* Vera Duckworth, that's for certain.

Nearby Liverpool will be familiar to most readers because of the Beatles. Liverpool English, known as Scouse (said to derive from the stew lobscouse, almost certainly a nativised form of the German dish *Labskaus*) is heavily influenced by Irish English, since so many Irish immigrants have settled in the city. As in Irish, New York or Caribbean English, th at the start of words like *those*, *things* and *there* can be pronounced with a *t* or *d*, so a pronunciation like *Dose tings dere* wouldn't be unusual. And *t* can often sound like *s* in Liverpool, so that *what* can sound like *woss*, and *back* gets a guttural *ch* sound at the end, winding up like German *Bach*. And *fur* and *fair* often sound alike in Liverpool. But just in case you thought this was getting too easy, sometimes Scouse *fair* sounds like *fur* (to rhyme with *stir*) and sometimes *fur* sounds like *fair* (to rhyme with *stair*). For some reason, Scouse gets a very hard time from speakers of other varieties of English – it's perhaps because the city has a very high crime rate by British standards, so that people elsewhere associate Liverpudlians – Scouse scallies – and their speech with car theft, pickpocketing and general dishonesty. Like Glaswegian, Scouse is regularly rated near the bottom of the scale of accent attractiveness and it's very difficult to shift these stereotypes once they're lodged in people's minds.

ACCENTS & DIALECTS

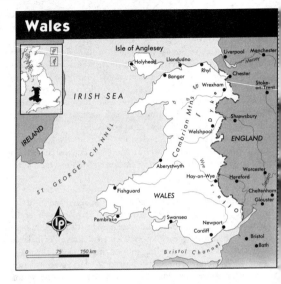

Wales

WALES

Wales, a principality accounting for an area around the size of Massachusetts, came under the control of the English king Edward I in the 12th century, and was formally united with England in 1535. Despite a policy of enforced anglicisation which was relaxed only within the last two or three generations, the Welsh language (see page 263) has managed to survive. For many Welsh people – particularly in the north and west of the country – English is spoken as a second language, and so the English of parts of Wales is heavily influenced by Welsh.

Welsh accents of English have features which make them rather like accents of England – h is frequently dropped, and r isn't pronounced in words like bird, other, or Cardiff. On the other hand, many Welsh English speakers use a decidedly un-English 'tapped r'. You can also hear Welsh people 'doubling' consonants in English words. Pat her thus doesn't sound the same as patter, for example – this is like the way that some Italian people follow the spelling and double the consonants in English words like cottage, adding, rubber, or gallon. The influence of Welsh is particularly noticeable in the case of intonation, which is carried over to give the English of many Welsh people a 'sing-song' quality.

bach/bachgen	term of endearment; a child (from the Welsh for 'small')
bad	ill/unwell
bailey	backyard; the gap between the front door and the gate of a house
cammit	crooked (from Welsh cam meaning 'crooked')
cwm	(pronounced *coom*) valley
lairy	weary/tired

WELSH ENGLISH

In Wales, expect to hear isn't it? (usually pronounced innit) quite a lot at the end of a sentence, regardless of the verb that went before it. That is, don't be surprised if people say things like 'We went to Newport last week-end, innit?' – again, this may be the influence of Welsh at work. Similarly, there's nothing odd in Welsh English about saying 'Where to's the hammer?', 'Where to are you going?' or 'Where's my wallet to?'. And you can switch the word order around in Welsh English, so that 'Hurt she was' or 'Awful I thought it sounded!' brings the injury or awfulness into sharper focus. The use of there's is also a bit different from Standard English – Welsh people can say 'There's lovely!' or 'There's cosy!' in the sense of 'That's lovely!' or 'How cosy!'.

lonk	hungry
lose	to miss
	He lost the bus.
mamgu	(pronounced *mamghee*) grandmother
mitch	play truant
mooch	see mitch
nain	(pronounced *nine*) see mamgu
off	hostile/angry
petty	toilet (also ty bach, from Welsh 'small house')
pilm	dust
pursy/putsy	easy
simple	ill/unwell
sorty	proud
tadchu	(pronounced *tadkey*) grandfather
taid	(pronounced *tide*) see tadchu
tidy	general term of approval. Can mean 'good-looking' she's a tidy girl, 'well done' a tidy job, or 'decent' a tidy sort of chap.
top room	sitting room
trwstan	(pronounced *troostan*) clumsy
tump	hill/mound, as in unty-tump, a molehill (from Welsh twmp)
twp	(pronounced *toop*) simple/slow-witted

The English spoken in Wales is also influenced a good deal by the dialects of the West Midlands of England, which lie just across Offa's Dyke, an ancient earthwork marking the border. But where Welsh English is by and large viewed fairly positively in other parts of Britain, Midland English is reviled by just about everyone, including the people who speak it.

West Midlands

1.	Wolverhampton
2.	Dudley
3.	Sandwell
4.	Walsall
5.	Birmingham
6.	Solihull
7.	Coventry

THE WEST MIDLANDS

The city of Birmingham – the largest in Britain after London – is the nerve centre of the West Midlands. But despite Birmingham's importance to the British economy, its inhabitants – known as Brummies – tend to get something of a bad press. As the saying goes, 'Brummie born and Brummie bred, strong in the arm and thick in the head'. The name Brummie derives from Brummagem (an alternative pronunciation of Birmingham), a word which – to make matters worse – has a second meaning the *Concise Oxford Dictionary* defines as 'counterfeit, cheap and showy'.

So what's wrong with Brum? Surely, there's nothing intrisically unattractive about the accent itself – as with Liverpool English it's probably got a good deal more to do with the negative perceptions of the heavily industrialised West Midlands themselves. The accent's not so very different from the accents of the rural – and very picturesque – counties of Staffordshire, Hereford & Worcester and Warwickshire, which surround the urban West Midlands. Brummies themselves will tell you that Birmingham English is beauty itself compared to the English spoken in the areas known as the Black Country (Dudley, Walsall, Wolverhampton) and the Potteries (Stoke-on-Trent), while Black Country and Potteries people say that Brum is just a watered-down version of 'true' Midlands dialect.

The expressions below may be heard generally around the Midlands, especially in Birmingham and in the Black Country.

adrenchen	soaking wet
am ya?	are you?
anent	against; next to
arsy	grumpy/moody
bab	baby/love/darling
backen	delay; keep back
bad	ill
bin	am
	Aa, I bin – Yes, I am.
bonk	small hill (see tacky-bonk)
Bostin!	Great!/Super!
cag-mag	a gossip
caggy-handed/ cass-handed	left-handed
chunter	mutter/mumble/grumble
clemmed/clammed	hungry
cob	bread roll
cob it	throw it away
cod	to joke
	Goo un, you'm coddin' me!

cost	can you? (negative – cosn't)
coost	could you? (negative – coosn't)
croggin' in	jumping the queue
cut	canal
donnies	hands (perhaps from French *donner*, 'to give')
fittle	food
frizoggled	freezing cold
gain	handy/skilful
got a nark on	annoyed (also got a monk on, got a bag on)
jed	dead (also jeth, 'death')
lief	as soon as
mash	to brew tea
mumchance	dolefully/dejectedly/bored
noggin	a thick slice of bread
pack o' saftness	a load of nonsense
pail	to beat
	I'll gi 'im a good pailin' when 'e cums whum.
peg it	to run away
pikelet	crumpet/muffin
pither	to potter about aimlessly
playing t'wag	playing truant
potch	to forestall
powk	a sty on the eye
reesty	rancid (of fat, butter or cheese)
robin dogs	cheated; ripped off
saft	silly/daft
shommock	to walk with a shuffling gait
skraze	to scratch/graze

starving	cold
suck	sweets
tacky-bonk	a pit mound (see bonk)
taff	to steal (perhaps from Taff, a nickname for a Welshman)
tararabit	(pronounced *tara-a-bit*) goodbye
tosh	moustache
twaggin' (it)	see playing t'wag
we	our We have we dinner.
Weer bist?	Where are you?
weld	to hit someone
welly	nearly Welly clemmed to jeth.
we'm	we are
wench	a girl (not derogatory – used by both males and females)
wozzer	Birmingham term for someone from the Black Country
yawl	bawl; shout; cry loudly
yawp	see yawl
you'm	you are
zowk	yelp; cry out

Some of the vowels of Birmingham English are 'lowered' – so me sounds like *may*, and you sounds like *yow*. Right and price are *roight* and *proice* (as in some Irish accents), the vowel of fate and tame can be more like that of 'fight' and 'time', and it, bid, rich can be mistaken for 'eat', 'bead' and 'reach'. Bus is pronounced more like *buzz*, and as in many urban accents of British English, h is dropped most of the time.

ACCENTS & DIALECTS

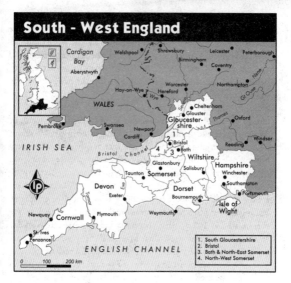

THE SOUTH-WEST OF ENGLAND

The south-western part of England is generally taken to mean the long arm of land extending from Hampshire, Wiltshire and Gloucestershire through Somerset and Dorset to Devon and finally Cornwall. The far western reaches of the Cornish peninsula are almost as distant from London as are the northern counties of Cumbria and Northumberland, and as a result the local speech has retained features of much earlier forms of English.

Cornwall English features a number of words from Cornish, an extinct Celtic language related to Welsh and Breton, but these are quite rare. Examples are fossick (to root around for something, as in 'She was fossicking around in my sock drawer'), clickyhanded (left-handed, from Cornish glikin, 'left'), clunk (to swallow) and whidden (runt or weakling, in a litter of pigs for example – from gwyn 'white'). Interestingly, the word penguin may derive from Cornish pen gwyn, 'white head', a term originally applied to the great auk of the North Atlantic, which looked, before it was hunted to extinction, a bit like the penguins of the southern hemisphere.

South-western English can sound a little like American English in that the r is pronounced in words like farmyard, Cornwall, or Somerset. It's like the accent that British people invariably adopt when they're trying to sound like a farmer or other yokel (country bumpkin, hick) – this stereotype is one of a rosy-cheeked simpleton dressed in a smock, chewing a straw, and hefting an earthenware crock of cider on his shoulder, occasionally saying 'Oo aar, oi loikes zoider, oi does', in a satisfied manner and spending the entire day leaning against a five-bar gate admiring the pastoral scene. If you've ever heard *The Archers*, BBC's perennial radio soap about 'everyday country folk', you'll know what I mean! But this stereotype goes a long way back. We can see clues as to the pronunciation of West Country English in Shakespeare's *King Lear*. Edgar, son of the Earl of Gloucester, has disguised himself as a 'peasant', and adopts an appropriate accent to complete the image. Ch 'ill is 'Ich will' (I will) – the 'Ich' looks like German, but was quite common in south-western parts into recent times.

> Ch'ill not let go, zir, without vurther 'casion ...
> Good gentleman, go your gait, and let poor volk pass
> An chud ha' bin zwaggered out of my life,
> 'twould not ha' bin zo long as 'tis by a vortnight.

You'll notice here that s becomes 'z' (zir, zwaggered, zo), and f becomes 'v' (vurther, volk, vortnight). This is still a feature of south-western English, which is why you can sometimes see the name Somerset written as Zummerzet. As in Birmingham, the vowel of tie becomes like that of 'toy'. Bread may rhyme with 'paid', mow with 'too' and hill with 'feel'. Sounds may switch with one another, so crisp is *crips*, clasp is *claps*, rich is *urch*, red is *urd* and yes is *ace*. Th can sound like *d* (*dree, droat*). And there are some remnants of older forms of English grammar such as baint (not going to, I baint – 'I won't'), er be (he is) and you bist (you are). *Mun* is them, as in I knawed mun well – 'I knew them well'.

The dialect words that follow are drawn from Devon English, though they can be found more widely across the south-west.

argify	to argue
assards	backwards
auncy	anxious
braxis	breakfast
casn	cannot
bay-spittle	honey (lit: bee-spit)
bird/burd	term of endearment, between either sex
caal	think
	What do ee caal you'm doing? –
	What do you think you're doing?
dane	red-haired man
drumbledrane	bumble bee
emmet	ant
galley	to frighten, alarm
	Did er galley you? –
	Did he frighten you?
grockle	holidaymaker/visitor
grubbish	hungry
kaky	sticky

laceing	huge
lacer	huge
mort	a lot
	There's a mort o' volk up church – There's a lot of people up at the church.
pitching	settling of snow
pluff	unwell
power	a lot
shrammed	to be cold
shug	shy
sketchy	strange/odd
spun out	angry
suent	smooth
tempt	to touch
	Doant ee tempt it! – Don't you touch it!
wee	exclamation of surprise
woppit	to box someone's ears
	Er geed un a woppit roun yurrole – He gave him a clout round the earhole.
yucks	hiccups
zog	to doze/snooze

A very odd feature of south-western English is the habit of either dropping the l from the end of words like angle, mackerel (*ango*, *macrow*) or putting an l in where originally there wasn't one (as in Bristol, formerly Bristow, the largest city in the south-west). The British linguist Peter Trudgill reports hearing of three Bristol sisters Evil, Idle, and Normal, while confusion can result when Bristolians ask people from the US about what life is like in a miracle. Think about it!

SLANG

The previous sections are just a sampler of the dozens of individual dialects in Britain, and as such have barely scratched the surface, but the broad groups listed in this chapter should at least give you some idea of what to expect. On top of traditional dialect, of course, there is slang. The latest expressions very often start life in London but spread outward with astonishing speed – TV and radio programmes popular with young people are probably instrumental in this spread, as are tabloid newspapers. The verb bonk, for instance (referring to sexual intercourse) appears to have begun life in newspaper headlines as a conveniently short and sanitary substitute for other relevant four-letter words, but has since passed into everyday use throughout the country. But increasingly, new slang terms are coming into British English from Australian and American English – not surprising, when you consider how young British people spend their spare time. The most popular TV programmes seem to be American and Australian. MTV is as popular in Britain as it is everywhere else in the world, and of course most of the films shown in British cinemas come from Hollywood – Quentin Tarantino films seem to be particularly influential in terms of introducing new slang – so many of the terms listed below will be familiar to Americans and Australians already.

bafta	good/cool
banging	enjoyable/fun
	We had a bangin' time last night.
bender	a drinking spree
black	good/cool
bod	unpopular and/or unfashionable person
class	good/cool/nice-looking
decent	good/cool/nice-looking

the dog's bollocks	fantastic
dork	unpopular and/or unfashionable person
doss	very easy That exam – what a doss!; money (also dosh)
draw	marijuana
drip	boring, unfashionable person
dweeb	unpopular and/or unfashionable person
fit	attractive/sexy
floss	to flirt
gear	recreational drugs
geek	as in American English, an unpopular and/or unfashionable person
gimp	see geek
goon	see geek
gross	disgusting/ugly/awful
jammy	lucky
jism/jissum/jissom	this can apparently mean just about anything, but most commonly means 'good' or 'cool' (it doesn't seem to have anything to do with bodily fluids!)
horizontal	cool/easy-going
horny	randy; attractive/sexy
kicking	enjoyable/fun
large	fun/cool Bob's party was well large.

larging (it)	having a good time at a party or club
lost it; lost the plot	confused/rambling
lush	good/tasty/attractive
minger	an ugly person
mint	attractive
moose	unpleasant/boring/ugly
naff	unfashionable; passé; poor quality
nerd	unpopular and/or unfashionable person
nugget	a £1 coin
pants	bad; an expletive Pants!
pillock	idiot/fool
pog	unpopular and/or unfashionable person
poo	bad; an expletive
puff	marijuana
rank	disgusting/ugly
rocks	cool/exciting Bungee jumping rocks!
sad	unfashionable He's a sad twat, him.
sadcase/saddo	an unfashionable person
safe	excellent/cool
screg	an unfashionable, badly-dressed person

shandy	someone who can't handle drink
sharp	attractive/sexy
skank	(n) an unfashionable, badly-dressed person; (v) to steal/cheat
skanky	ugly/smelly/dirty/foul
skeg	an unfashionable, badly-dressed person
smart	good/cool/fashionable
sorted	good/cool/fashionable. Can also mean to have scored drugs. You sorted for Es?
sound	good/cool/fashionable
stomping	enjoyable/fun
sucky	dull/bad
tax	to steal
top	excellent/cool
twat	(n) an idiot; (v) to strike/hit/punch
twoc	to steal a car, go joyriding (probably an acronym for 'Take Without Consent')
well	very Let's go to Club X – the music's well good.
whizz	speed (amphetamines)
wicked	excellent/cool/exciting
wonga	money

Drunk Again ...

arseholed, battered, bevvied (up), bladdered, blootered,
bollocksed, bricked, buckled, buttwhipped, cabbaged,
caned, creamed, crushed, cunted, floored, fucked, guttered,
hammered, hamstered, kalied, kaly, knackered, lashed,
leathered, leery, legless, mashed, monged, mortal,
mortalled, off it, off one's face, off one's trolley, out of
one's face, out of one's head, out of one's tree, pallatic,
para, paralytic, pished, pissed (as a fart, as a newt), plonked,
rat-arsed, ratted, reeling, scoobied, shedded, shitfaced,
slashed, slaughtered, slewed, sloshed, sozzled, steaming,
stotted, tanked, tankered, tired, trolleyed, wankered,
wasted, wazzed, well gone, wellied, wrecked

While we're on the subject, here are some choice expressions for
vomiting.

barf, blow, blow chunks, blow one's groceries, boak, chak,
chuck, chunder, flurg, heave, have a technicolor yawn, hurl,
lose one's lunch, make a pavement pizza, pray to the
porcelain god, razz, retch, throw (up), vom, yak

And of course these lists would be incomplete without the
necessary terminology for the after-effects of drinking to excess.
A number of these, oddly, are the same as terms for drunk.

badly, bollocksed, bombed, buckled, busted, delicate,
fragile, fucked, got by the Beer Monster, jaded, knackered,
minged, monged, paying it, rough, struggling, trashed

We could spend another whole chapter on slang terms that are
common knowledge among young people but pretty obscure to
older ones – words to do with current sporting fashions

(snowboarding, mountain biking, rollerblading and street hockey), to do with recreational drugs, pop music, and sex. And no doubt anyone using this guide will, very quickly, be able to find dozens of slang terms not included here. Slang comes in and goes out of fashion so quickly that if you try out some of the above expressions on a young British person he or she may well respond, 'Plonked? Skanky? That's sooooooo 1999! Get with it, will you?'.

What with all this diversity and constant change in British English, you're probably wondering how you're going to get by at all, even if you're a native speaker. Well, don't worry – it's a lot easier than you'd think. Because in Britain we're exposed to other forms of English (especially American English) from a very early age, the average Brit is more 'bidialectal' than his or her American counterpart, and may very well know the American word for such-and-such a thing or concept. The point of this chapter has been to help you to enjoy the wealth of accent and dialect we have on our small island. You don't have to be a linguist or a dialectologist to become absorbed in it – it's there for anyone to investigate – and in general, speakers of unusual or unfamiliar dialects will be more than happy to spend time talking to you about their own particular variety (sometimes, in fact, it can be hard to get them to button their lip, haud their whisht or belt up!) True, British English can sometimes be baffling. But it is genuinely, and endlessly, fascinating.

SCOTTISH GAELIC

INTRODUCTION

Scottish Gaelic (Gàidhlig, pronounced *Gah-lik*) is spoken by about 66,000 people, mainly in the traditional Gaelic-speaking areas of the Highlands and Islands in the west and north west of Scotland. All speakers are bilingual in Gaelic and English. Migration during the present and last century, mainly due to socio-economic factors, has meant that increasing numbers now live in or near large urban areas such as Glasgow and Edinburgh. For similar reasons, Scottish Gaelic was introduced in the 19th century to Nova Scotia (Canada) where it is still spoken to this day.

Scottish Gaelic belongs to the Goedelic branch of Celtic. Irish (Gaeilge) spoken in Ireland, and Manx (Gaelg), a language formerly spoken on the Isle of Man that's recently been revived, are closely related to Scottish Gaelic.

Gaelic wasn't the first language spoken in Scotland – Scotland was home to a set of tribes called Picts who spoke a language or set of languages usually referred to as Pictish. It's generally believed that Gaelic was brought to Scotland by Irish settlers some time before the 5th century AD. The Romans called these settlers Scotti (literally 'Irishmen'), which later gave rise to the country's name. By the 11th and 12th centuries, Gaelic was spoken in most parts of modern Scotland and place names give ample evidence of this (see page 254).

Due to geographical factors and contacts with different cultures such as the Picts, the Britons, the Vikings and the Anglo-Saxons, Scottish Gaelic gradually began to diverge from the mother language Irish. Despite this divergence, the Gaels of Ireland and Scotland were united by a common literary language, adopted during the Classical period (1200-1700), in which the bards composed poetry for their patrons. This literary standard tended to obscure, if not diminish, some of the dissimilarities which had developed in the vernacular language. The various cultural influences on Scottish Gaelic can to some degree be measured by the 'borrowed' placenames in Scottish Gaelic.

The decline of Scottish Gaelic began with the anglicisation of the Scottish dynasty, and the establishment of English-speaking burghs from roughly the 12th century in the Lowlands of Scotland (in eastern and central Scotland). The Scottish court spoke English and Norman-French, and the northern dialect of English (Inglis) replaced Gaelic as the official language. Trading with these burghs led to the eventual spread of English and the gradual demise of Gaelic in outlying Lowland areas. The Lordship of the Isles, founded in the mid-12th century, and partly based on the earlier Norse kingdom of the Western and Southern Isles, became an important focus and centre of Gaelic culture and learning. This continued until the late 15th century when the Lordship was destroyed by the central authorities of Scotland. All of the above factors together served to reduce the formerly high status of Gaelic in Scottish society.

Meanwhile, Gaelic flourished as a vernacular in the Highlands and Islands right up to the 18th century, the time of the Jacobite rebellions and wars. Following the Battle of Culloden in 1746, the Gaels were punished for their involvement in these wars by a variety of measures including the banning of traditional costumes and music. One of the most drastic measures taken against the Gaels, which was nothing less than a process of ethnic cleansing conducted by landlords and various governments, gave rise to what are normally called the Highland Clearances (na Fuadaitchean) of the 19th century. After realising that sheep were more profitable than tenants, some landlords drove the Gaels from their ancestral lands and homes, with many of them ending up in far-away lands such as Canada. Needless to say, the Clearances delivered a severe blow to the Gaelic language in Scotland. However, the 1872 Education Act (Scotland), which imposed a national system of education, largely destroyed the Gaelic school system set up by religious groups in the 19th century. Through a mixture of malice and ignorance, under the new regime the use of Gaelic was actively discouraged in schools, which helped strip Gaelic of much of its social prestige.

Efforts to revive and restore Gaelic began in the later 19th century, and significant progress has been made especially since the 1970s, most notably in the areas of education and the media. Teaching in the Gaelic language has expanded considerably in the past two decades both in traditional areas and in cities, with more than 2000 children taught in Gaelic, and some subjects taught at secondary level. Gaelic is taught (usually within Departments of Celtic) in Scotland's four main universities. The Gaelic College on the Isle of Skye, Sabhal Mór Ostaig, conducts a wide variety of tertiary-level courses in Gaelic, and has recently begun to offer degree courses.

Hundreds of hours of Gaelic television programming is broadcast every year, and Gaelic radio station Radio nan Gàidheal broadcasts regularly. Scotland has a Gaelic newspaper and Gaelic articles appear regularly in some national and regional weekly newspapers. The Government has recently agreed to sign the European Charter for Minority Languages, which should ensure a measure of security for the language in the future.

All of these developments have served to raise the profile of Gaelic, and more importantly to increase the confidence of speakers in their language and culture. The tide has turned.

GUIDE TO TRANSLITERATIONS

A simplified phonetic transliteration has been included alongside Scottish Gaelic words, and Welsh words in the next chapter, to give an additional guide to their pronunciation. The following system has been used for transliterations. Syllables that have been bolded indicate stress.

Vowels

a	as the 'a' in 'bat'
ah	as the 'a' in 'father'
e	as the 'e' in 'bet'
eh	as the 'a' in 'scare'
o	as the 'o' in 'hot'
oo	as the 'oo' in 'food'
oe	as the 'u' in 'burn'
u	as the 'oo' in 'good'
uh	as the 'u' in 'cut'

Diphthongs

ai	as the 'i' in 'dive'
ay	as the 'ay' in 'play'
aw	as the 'aw' in 'thaw'
ea	as the 'ea' in 'near'
oh	as the 'oa' in 'boat'
ow	as the 'ow' in 'vow'
uey	as the 'uey' in 'chop suey'

Consonants

y	as the 'y' in 'yacht'
j	as the 'j' in 'joke'
ch	as the 'ch' in 'chimpanzee'
zh	as the 's' in 'pleasure'
th	as the 'th' in 'thin'
th	as the 'th' in 'these'
kh	as the 'ch' in Scottish 'loch' or German 'ich'
gh	similar to *kh* except the sound is voiced
ky	as the 'cu' sound in 'acute'
by	as the 'beau' in 'beauty'
ly	as the 'lli' in 'batallion'
ny	as the 'ni' in 'onion'
ry	like an 'r' sound followed by a 'y' sound
rr	trilled 'r' as in Spanish 'burro'

PRONUNCIATION

Unlike English, the stress in Scottish Gaelic almost always falls on the first syllable of a word. Even the word poileas (borrowed from English 'police') is stressed on the first syllable. Although Scottish Gaelic spelling may seem complicated, it's in fact more regular than that of English, and pronunciation becomes easier once you're familiar with the spelling system. Gaelic uses only 18 letters in its alphabet (j, k, q, v, w, x, y, z aren't generally used). Despite having fewer letters, Scottish Gaelic actually has more individual sounds than English with the 'extra' sounds represented by various combinations of the 18 letters.

Vowels

Accents are used to indicate long vowels. Grave accents (è) are the norm nowadays although some writers also use acute accents (é) with the vowels e and o to indicate vowels of a different quality. Compare short a in cas 'foot' with long à in càs 'difficulty'. Vowels fall into two groups:

a, o, u	broad vowels
i, e	slender vowels

Vowels are combined in various ways to represent different vowel sounds, some of which don't occur in English. The help of a native speaker is invaluable for these. The less obvious ones are:

eu	as the 'ee' in 'free' followed by a short 'ah' sound (beul *bee-ahl* 'mouth')
	as the 'a' in 'shame' (Seumas *shaym-uhs* 'James')
ao	as the 'oo' in 'food' but with unrounded lips

Consonants

Only the consonants l, n and r may be doubled, to ll, nn and rr. These double consonants are generally longer than the single ones.

Broad & Slender Consonants

All consonants except h have two pronunciations, one broad, the other slender.

Broad consonants are pronounced approximately as in English, although t and d (and l(l), nn) are pronounced with the tongue against the teeth. A broad s is always pronounced as the 's' in 'song', never as the 's' in 'pleasure'.

Slender consonants have an inbuilt 'y' sound which can be approximated by placing a 'y' sound after the sound.

| beò | *byow* | alive |
| ceò | *kyow* | smoke/mist |

SLENDER CONSONANTS

c	always pronounced as the 'c' in 'cat', never as an 's' sound
d	as the 'j' in 'judge'
t	as the 'ch' in 'cheek'
s	as the 'sh' in 'shoe'
l(l)	as the 'lli' in 'million'
n(n)	as the 'ny' in 'canyon'
r	varies among dialects, and has no English equivalent. Can sound something like the 'th' in 'these'.

When a consonant comes next to, or is surrounded by broad vowels, the consonant is said to be broad. When next to or surrounded by a slender vowel, a consonant is said to be slender. A fundamental spelling rule of Scottish Gaelic is that 'broad goes with broad, and slender with slender' – when a consonant is preceded by a broad vowel it must be followed by a broad vowel and when it's preceded by a slender vowel it must be followed by a slender vowel.

balach   'a boy'   caileag   'a girl'

In the latter example the i and e aren't pronounced – they merely indicate that the l is to be pronounced as a slender l.

The Letter 'h'

The letter h can occur before a vowel or be added to the letters b, c, d, f, g, m, p, s and t to provide a new set of softened sounds. This process, called lenition, operates at all levels of the language, and is an important aspect of Celtic languages. Lenition is associated with feminine nouns.

bh	as the 'v' in 'voice'
mh	as the 'v' in 'voice'
ch	when broad, like 'ch' in Scottish 'loch'; when slender like 'ch' in German 'ich' (never pronounced as 'ch' in 'cheek')
dh	when broad, the voiced version of broad ch, which sounds like a French or German 'r' made at the back of the throat; when slender, as the 'y' in 'yes'
gh	see dh
ph	as the 'f' in 'finger'
fh	silent
sh	as the 'h' in 'horse'

th	as the 'h' in 'horse'
r	when broad, like the 'r' in 'rock'; when slender, has no English equivalent, but in some dialects can sound like the 'th' in 'then'

Sounds occurring anywhere in a word can undergo lenition, and when this happens at the beginning of a word, it's usually due to the influence of the previous word.

The words for 'her' and 'his' look the same – they're both a, but yet are fundamentally different. When the word a means 'his', an 'h' is added to the next word, which makes the first letter softer. The word a, 'her', doesn't affect a following consonant.

a cù			a chù	
uh koo	her dog		*uh khoo*	his dog
a beul			a bheul	
uh bee-al	her mouth		*uh vee-al*	his mouth

GRAMMAR

Here's a brief description of some of the more important characteristics of Scottish Gaelic grammar.

Word Order

Unlike English, word order in Scottish Gaelic is usually verb-subject-object.

I'd like some red wine.	Bu toigh leam fìon dearg. (lit: like wine red)

Nouns

Nouns in Scottish Gaelic are either masculine or feminine.

òran (m)		craobh (f)	
o-ran	song	*kroov*	tree

Plurals

The plural of some masculine nouns is formed by adding **i** before the final consonant. This can change the preceding vowel.

cat *kat*	cat	cait *kach*	cats
Gàidheal *ge-yul*	Gael	Gàidheil *ge-ily*	Gaels
cnoc *krok*	hill	cnuic *kru-iky*	hills

For all other nouns, it's formed by adding an ending containing **-an**.

caileag *ka-lak*	girl	caileagan *ka-la-kun*	girls
baile *ba-luh*	town	bailtean *bal-chun*	towns
àite *aa-chuh*	place	àitichean *aa-chi-khin*	places
latha *lah-uh*	day	lathaichean *lah-i-khin*	days
ainm *a-nam*	name	ainmean *a-na-mun*	names

Articles

Scottish Gaelic has no indefinite article (a/an), so that balach can mean 'boy' or 'a boy' and caileagan can mean 'girls' or 'some girls'. The definite article an 'the' precedes the noun. When the article is used with nouns that are feminine, the first sound of the noun becomes softer, and the article is spelled a'.

an duine (m) *un du-nyuh*	the man	a' chaileag (f) *uh kha-lak*	the girl

SCOTTISH GAELIC

an càr (m)   a' Ghàidhlig (f)
un kaar the car   *uh ghaa-lik* the Gaelic

When the article an appears with a masculine noun that begins with a vowel, t- is added to the noun.

an t-uisge (m)   an obair (f)
un tush-kyuh the water   *un o-biry* the work

an t-aiseag (m)   an uinneag (f)
un tash-uk the ferry   *un u-nyak* the window

When the article appears with a feminine noun that begins with s, t- is added to the noun and the s isn't pronounced.

an solas (m)   an t-sràid (f)
un so-lus the light   *un traaj* the street

Before masculine nouns beginning with b, f, p and m, the article an becomes am.

am balach   am baile
um ba-lukh the boy   *um ba-luh* the town

POSSESSIVE FORMS OF THE DEFINITE ARTICLE

For singular nouns, the possessive forms of the definite articles are:

Before masculine nouns:

a' + *lenition* or an before consonants
an before vowels
an t- before s

Before feminine nouns:

na before consonants
na h- before vowels

The article used with the possessive plural is nan or nam.

These forms are common in placenames.

Gaelic form	Anglified form	
Baile a' Chaolais	Ballachulish	the town of the narrows
Baile a' Mhonaidh	Ballymoney	the town of the moor
Cill an Iubhair	Killineuar	the church of the yew
Taigh an Uillt	Taynuilt	the house of the stream
Pit na Craoibhe	Pitnacree	the portion/farm of the tree
Tom na h-Iubhraich	Tomnahurich	knoll of the yew
Loch nan Eala	Lochnell	the loch of the swans

Adjectives

Adjectives in Scottish Gaelic usually follow the noun, the most important exception being seann 'old' which precedes the noun, seann duine 'old man', seann taigh 'old house'. When an adjective follows a feminine noun, the first sound becomes softer.

latha (m)	*la-uh*	day
latha math (m)	*lah-huh mah*	a good day
oidhche (f)	*aikh-uh*	night
oidhche mhath (f)	*aikh-uh vah*	a good night

Possession

An idea of the way possession is expressed in Scottish Gaelic is useful for understanding Scottish placenames. The thing possessed is followed by its possessor.

SCOTTISH GAELIC

James' house.	taigh Sheumais.
	(lit: house James)
The carpenter's town.	baile an t-saoir.
	(lit: town the carpenter)

Pronouns

There are two sets of personal pronouns in Scottish Gaelic – a 'normal' set and a 'contrastive' set used to contrast and emphasise.

	Normal	Contrastive
I	mi	mise
	mee	*mee-shuh*
you	thu/tu	thusa/tusa
	oo/doo	*oo-suh/doo-suh*
he/it (m)	e	esan
	eh	*e-san*
she/it (f)	i	ise
	ee	*ee-shuh*
we	sinn	sinne
	shiny	*shi-nyuh*
you (pl/pol)	sibh	sibhse
	shiv	*siv-shuh*
they	iad	iadsan
	at	*at-sun*

DEMONSTRATIVES

this	seo	sho
that (near)	sin	shin
that (distant)	siud	shit
here	an-seo	iuh sho
there (near)	an-sin	uh shin
there (distant)	an-siud	uh shit

Verbs
To Be

There are two verbs meaning 'to be' in Scottish Gaelic – tha and is. The verb is is used in sentences where a noun follows the verb 'to be'. In other cases the verb tha is used.

John's cold.
Tha Iain fuar.   *ha ee-any foo-ar*

You're Mary.
Is tusa Màiri.   *sdoo-suh maar-yee*

The contrastive/emphatic pronouns are used with the verb is. However, both the regular and the contrastive pronouns can be used with the verb tha to give a different meaning.

I'm tired.
Tha mi sgìth.   *ha mee skee*

I am tired also
Tha mise sgìth cuideachd.   *ha mee-shuh skee*
(mise adds contrast or   *kuch-ukhk*
emphasis)

If the object of the verb isn't a proper noun or doesn't appear with an article, a different construction is used.

I'm a doctor.   'Se dotair a tha annam.
     (lit: it's a doctor that is in-me)

You're a Gael.   'Se Gàidheal a tha annad.
     (lit: it's a Gael that is in-you)

Present Tense

The present tense of tha is formed as follows:

I drink/I'm drinking.   Tha mi ag òl.
     (lit: am I at drinking)

I go/I'm going.	Tha mi a' dol.	
	(lit: am I at going)	

Note that ag 'at' becomes a' before consonants.

I'm ...	Tha mi ...	*ha mee ...*
eating	ag ithe	*gyi-huh*
travelling	a' siubhal	*shoo-yul*

The preposition ann, meaning 'in' and the personal
pronouns combine to form one word.

annam	in-me	ann	in-him/it
annad	in-you	innte	in-her

Past Tense

The past tense of tha is bha, the negative form is cha robh and
the question form is an robh.

John was sick.	
Bha Iain tinn.	*va ee-any cheen*

Mary wasn't there.	
Cha robh Màiri ann.	*kha ro maa-ryee own*

Were you at the ceilidh/dance?	
An robh thu aig a' chéilidh?	*un ro oo eky uh khe-lee*

To Have

Scottish Gaelic doesn't have a verb that's equivalent to the verb 'to
have' in English. Instead, the verb tha is used together with the
preposition aig 'at'.

Anna has a cat.	Tha cat aig Anna.
	(lit: is a cat at Anna)

Aig also combines with the personal pronouns.

agam	at-me	aige	at-him
agad	at-you	aice	at-her

I have a cat.

Tha cat agam.
(lit: is cat at-me)

You have a dog.

Tha cù agad.
(lit: is dog at-you)

He has money.

Tha airgead aige.
(lit: is money at-him)

She has a car.

Tha càr aice.
(lit: is car at-her)

INSULTS

Shut your mouth!
    Dùn do bheul!   *doon duh bheal!*
Get lost!
    Fhalbh!   *hala!*
Misfortune on you.
    Dunaidh ort.   *du-nai orsht*
Bad luck to you.
    Gonadh ort.   *go-nugh orsht*
Bad cess (luck) to you.
    Gum bu h-olc dhut.   *gu-muh holk ghuht*
You fool.
    A amadain.   *a-ma-tany*
You idiot.
    A ghloidhc.   *uh ghlaichk*

SCOTTISH GAELIC

To Know

One way of saying 'to know' is 'knowledge is at a person', meaning a person 'has knowledge'.

Anna knows.   Tha fios aig Anna.
        (lit: is knowledge at Anna)

I know.   Tha fios agam.
        (lit: is knowledge at-me)

Negatives

The verb tha 'to be' is negated by replacing it with chan eil.

Anna's not here.
 Chan eil Anna an-seo. *khany el a-nuh uh sho*

I don't know
 Chan eil fios agam. *khany el fees a-kum*

YES & NO

There are no single words in Scottish Gaelic that mean 'yes' or 'no'. Instead the verb of the question is 'echoed'.

Do you have time?
 Am bheil ùine agad? *uh vel oo-nyuh a-kut?*

Are you happy?
 An bheil sibh   *uh vel shiv*
 toilichte?   *to-lich-chuh?*

Yes.   Tha.
No.   Chan eil.

Questions

Tha sentences are made into questions by replacing the verb tha with am bheil.

Are you tired?
Am bheil thu sgìth?   *uh vel oo skee?*

Do you know?
Am bheil fios agad?   *uh vel fees a-kut?*

MEETING PEOPLE
You Should Know

Thank you. (sg inf)
Tapadh leat.   *ta-puh laht*

Thank you. (pl; sg pol)
Tapadh leibh.   *ta-puh laiv*

Thanks.
Taing.   *tah-eeng*

Many thanks.
Móran taing.   *moe-ran tah-eeng*

	sg inf	pl; sg pol
Please.	Mas e do thoil e. *ma-sheh duh hol eh*	Mas e ur toil e. *ma-sheh ur tol eh*
You're welcome.	'Se do bheatha. *shey duh veh-huh*	'Se ur beatha. *shey ur beh-huh*
Excuse me.	Gabh mo lethsgeul. *ga-muh lyesh-kyal*	Gabhaibh mo lethsgeul. *ga-iv muh lyesh-kyal*

SCOTTISH GAELIC

I'm sorry.	Tha mi duilich.	*ha mee doo-leech*
Yes.	Is toil.	*is tul*
No.	Cha toil.	*cha tul*

Come along/on.
  Trobhad.   *tro-ut*
Let's go.
  Thugainn.   *hu-kiny*
Go on./Continue.
  Siubhad.   *shoo-ut*
Oh dear!
  A chiall!   *uh kheal!*
Yuck!
  A ghia!   *uh yee-a!*
Goodness me!
  A thiarcais fhéin!   *uh hear-kish hen!*
Dear me!
  Obh obh!   *ov ov!*
  Mo chreach!   *muh khrakh!*
Pardon me.
  (Dé) b'àill leibh.   *(je) baal laiv*
Excuse me.
  Gabh mo lethsgeul.   *ga muh lyesh-kyal*
I don't mind.
  Tha mi coma.   *ha mee ko-muh*

Greetings & Goodbyes

Scottish Gaelic has no word that directly corresponds to 'hello'. Instead people greet one another by asking how they are and making comments on the weather, although expressions based on English idioms are becoming more common.

How are you?
Ciamar a tha thu/sibh?   *kemur uh ha oolshiv?*

Well.
Tha gu math.   *ha guh mah*

Not bad.
Chan eil dona.   *chany el donuh*

Good morning.
Madainn mhath.   *matiny vah*

Good afternoon/evening.
Feasgar math.   *feskur mah*

Good night.
Oidhche mhath.   *ai-khuh vah*

It's a lovely day.
Tha latha brèagha ann.   *ha lah-uh bree-a-uh own*

It's cold today.
Tha e fuar an-diugh.   *ha eh foo-ar un joo*

It's raining.
Tha an t-uisge ann.   *ha un tush-kyeh own*

It's snowing.
Tha sneachd ann.   *ha snyakh-kuh own*

It's misty.
Tha ceò ann.   *ha kyo own*

Goodbye. (inf) (lit: blessing with you)
Beannachd leat.   *byan-nukhk laht*

Goodbye. (pl; sg pol)
Beannachd leibh.   *byan-nukhk laiv*

Goodbye. (inf) (lit: the same to you)
Mar sin leat.   *mar shin laht*

Goodbye. (pol)
Mar sin leibh.   *mar shin laiv*

When addressing someone in Gaelic, a is placed before the name, which corresponds to English 'hey!'. The letter h is also added after the first letter of the name.

| A Mhàiri. | *uh va-ryee* | (Hey) Mary. |
| A Mhórag. | *uh voe-rak* | (Hey) Morag. |

If the person is male, an i is added before the final sound of the man's name.

| A Sheumais. | *uh Hay-mish* | (Hey) James. (this is where the name 'Hamish' comes from) |
| A Dhomhnaill. | *uh ghoe-ily* | (Hey) Donald. |

Making Conversation

What's your name? (inf)
Dé an t-ainm a tha ort?   *jen ta-nam a horsht?*

What's your name? (pol)
Dé an t-ainm a tha oirbh?   *jen ta-nam a hu-ryuf?*

Who are you?
Có thusa?   *coe oo-suh?*

| I'm … | Is mise … | *smee-shuh …* |

Do you speak Gaelic?
Am bheil Gàidhlig agad/agaibh?   *uh vel gaa-lik a-kut/a-kif?*

Yes, a little.
Tha beagan.   *ha be-kan*

Not much.
Chan eil móran.   *chany el moe-ran*

I'm learning.
Tha mi ag ionnsachadh.   *ha mee go-sukh-ugh*

What's this in Gaelic?
Dé tha seo anns a' Ghàidhlig? *je ha sho owns uh ghaa-lik?*

What do you like doing?
Dé as toil leat/leibh a
bhith a' dèanamh?
(inf/pol)
*jes tul laht/laiv uh vih uh
dee-anuv?*

Do you like sport?
An toil leat/leibh
spòrs? (inf/pol)
un tul laht/laiv sporsh?

Do you like drama?
An toil leat/leibh
dràma? (inf/pol)
un tul laht/laiv draa-muh?

What kind of music do you like?
Dé an seòrsa ciùil as
toil leat/leibh? (inf/pol)
*jen shor-shuh kyoo-il is tul
laht/laiv?*

Do you have any children?
Am bheil clann agad/
agaibh? (inf/pol)
uh vel klown a-kut/a-kif?

Do you have a partner?
Am bheil céile agad/
agaibh? (inf/pol)
uh vel keluh a-kut/a-kif?

Do you like ...?
An toil leat ...?
an tul laht ...?

SEASONS

Spring	an t-Earrach	*un tcha-rruch*
Summer	an Samhradh	*un sow-rugh*
Autumn	am Foghar	*um fu-ur*
Winter	an Geamhradh	*un gyow-rugh*

I like ...
   Is toil leam ...   *stul lum ...*

I don't like ...
   Cha toil leam ...   *cha tul lum ...*

I'd like ...
   Bu toil leam ...   *buh tul lum ...*

I wouldn't like ...
   Cha bu toil leam ...   *cha buh tul lum ...*

Would you like ...?
   Am bu toil leat ...?   *um buh tul laht ...?*

| Yes. | Bu toil. | *buh tul* |
| No. | Cha bu toil. | *cha buh tul* |

CONGRATULATIONS!

Happy Birthday!
   Co-latha breith   *koe lah-uh breh*
   sona dhut!   *so-nuh ghuht!*

Happy Christmas!
   Nollaig Chridheil!   *no-lik chree-al!*

Happy New Year!
   Bliadhna Mhath Ùr!   *blu-nuh vah oor!*

Congratulations! (inf/pol)
   Meal do/ur naidheachd!   *myal duh/ur ne-yachk!*

Cheers!
   Slàinte mhath!   *slaan-tchuh vah!*

Good luck. (inf/pol)
   Gun téid leat/leibh.   *gun jej laht/laiv*

Good luck. (inf/pol)
   Gun soirbhich leat/leibh. *gun so-ro-vich laht/laiv*

Happy birthday!
   Co-latha breith   *ko lah-uh breh*
   sona dhut!   *so-nuh ghuht!*

Going Out

What are you doing this evening?

| Dé tha thu/sibh a' dèanamh feasgar? (inf/pol) | je ha oo/shiv uh jee-a-nuv fes-gur? |

Would you like to go for a drink?

| Am bu toil leat/leibh a dhol a ghabhail drama? (inf/pol) | um buh tul laht/laiv uh ghol uh gha-al dra-muh? |

Would you like to go for a meal?

| Am bu toil leat/leibh a dhol gu biadh? (inf/pol) | um bu tul laht/laiv a ghol guh beagh? |

That'd be great.

| Bhiodh sin sgoinneil. | vee-ugh shin sku-nyal |

I'm sorry, I can't.

| Tha mi duilich, chan urrainn dhomh. | ha mee du-likh khan u-rriny gho |

Language Difficulties

I don't understand.

| Chan eil mi a' tuigsinn. | khany el mee tuky-shiny |

Could you say that again?

| An canadh tu/sibh sin a-rithist? (inf/pol) | un ka-nuh doo/shiv shin uh ryee-ishch? |

Could you speak more slowly please?

| Am bruidhneadh tu ar do shocair mas e do thoil e? (inf) | um bru-ee-nuh doo ery duh hoh-kiry ma-sheh duh hol eh? |
| Am bruidhneadh sibh ar ur socair mas e ur toil e? (pol) | um bru-ee-nuh shiv ery ur soh-kiry ma-sheh ur tol eh? |

SCOTTISH GAELIC

AROUND TOWN

I want to go to the ...

Tha mi ag iarraidh a	*ha mee gea-ree uh*	
dhol do ...	*ghol duh ...*	

Where's the ...?	Càite am bheil ...?	*kaa-chuh vel ...?*
airport	am port adhar	
bank	am banca	*um bang-kuh*
church	an eaglais	*un ek-lish*
cinema	an taigh-dhealbh	*un tai ya-lav*
ferry	an taiseag	*un ta-shuk*
hotel/pub	an taigh-òsda	*un tai os-tuh*
library	an leabharlann	*un lyo-ur-lann*
post office	oifis a' phuist	*o-fish uh fushch*
shop(s)	a' bhùth(an)	*uh voo(un)h*
station	an stèisean	*un ste-shan*
swimming pool	an t-amar snàmh	*un ta-mur snaav*
toilet	an taigh-beag	*an taigh-beag*
tourist inform-	ionad fiosrachaidh	*in-ut fees-rukh-*
ation centre	luchd turais	*ee lukhk tu-rish*
town centre	meadhan a' bhaile	*mee-an uh va-luh*

It's ...	Tha e ...	*ha eh ...*
here	an-seo	*uh sho*
there	an-sin	*uh shin*
over there (distant)	an-siud	*uh shit*
over there	thall an-sin	*howl uh shin*
up there	shuas an-sin	*hoo-as uh shin*

SCOTTISH GAELIC

over there (distant)	an-siud	*uh shit*
down there	shìos an-sin	*heas uh shin*
near the shop	faisg air a' bhùth	*fashky ery uh voo*
past the bank	seachad air a' bhanca	*sha-khut ery uh vang-kuh*

SIGNS

TAIGH-TASGAIDH	MUSEUM
POILEAS	POLICE
SRÀID A' PHRIONNSA	PRINCES STREET
SRÀID	STREET
IONADFÀILTEACHAIDH	RECEPTION
FON	TELEPHONE
TAIGH-BEAG	TOILET
FIR	MEN
MNATHAN	WOMEN
IONAD-FIOSRACHAIDH	TOURIST INFORMATION CENTRE
FÀILTE GU ...	WELCOME TO ...
CEUD MÌLE FÀILTE	A HUNDRED THOUSAND WELCOMES

Placenames

Barra
   Barraidh *ba-rrai*

Edinburgh (lit: the fort of Éideann)
   Dùn Éideann *dun e-junn*

Fort William (lit: the Garrison)
   An Gearrasdan *un gyer-a-stan*

Glasgow
   Glaschu *gla-sa-khoo*

Harris
   na Hearadh *nuh he-rugh*

the Highlands (lit: the place of the Gaels)
   a' Ghàidhealtachd *uh ghe-yul-takhk*

Inverness (lit: the outlet of Ness)
   Inbhir Nis *iny-or nyish*

the Isle of Skye
   An t-Eilean Sgitheanach *un che-lan skee-a-nukh*

Lewis
   Leódhas *lyoe-us*

Oban (lit: the small bay)
   An t-Òban *un to-ban*

Portree (lit: the harbour of the king)
   Port Rìgh *porsht ru-i*

Scotland
   Alba *a-la-puh*

Uist
   Uibhist *u-isch*

FOOD & DRINK

breakfast	bracaist	*bra-kishch*
dinner	dìnnear	*jee-nary*
drink	deoch	*jokh*
food	biadh	*beagh*
restaurant	taigh-bidhe/biadhlann	*tai bee-i/bea-ghlan*

What do you want?
  Dé tha thu ag iarraidh? *je ha oo gea-ree?*

Give me ... please.
  Thoir dhomh ... mas e   *hory gho ... ma-sheh*
  do thoil e.   *duh hol eh*

I'd like ...
  tha mi ag iarraidh   *ha mee gea-ree*

Are you hungry?
  Am bheil an t-acras ort? *uh vel an tak-rus orsht?*

Are you thirsty?
  Am bheil am pathadh ort? *uh vel um pah-ugh orsht?*

I'm hungry. (lit: the hunger is on me)
  Tha an t-acras orm.   *han tak-rus orom*

I'm thirsty. (lit: the thirst is on me)
  Tha am pathadh orm.   *ham pah-ugh o-rom*

'ON'

The preposition air 'on' combines with the pronouns.

on me	orm	*or-om*
on you	ort	*orsht*
on you (pol)	oirbh	*u-ryuf*
on him	air	*ery*
on her	oirre	*orr-uh*
on us	oirnn	*orny*
on them	orra	*orr-uh*

SCOTTISH GAELIC

I enjoyed that.
Chòrd sin rium. *chorsht shin ryum*

That was tasty.
Bha sin blasta. *va shin bla-stuh*

That was really tasty.
Bha sin deagh bhlasta. *va shin joe vla-stuh*

I'd like some more.
Tha mi ag iarraidh tuilleadh. *ha mee gearee too-lyugh*

Food

beans	pònair	*po-nary*
black pudding	marag dhubh	*ma-rak ghoo*
bread	aran	*a-ran*
butter	ìm	*eem*
carrot	curran	*ku-rran*
cheese	càise	*kyark*
chicken	cearc	*kyark*
crab	crùbag	*kroo-pak*
dessert	mìlsean	*meel-shan*
egg	ugh	*u*
eggs	uighean	*u-yun*
fish	iasg	*eask*
meat	feòil	*fyol*
oatcake(s)	aran-coirce	*a-ran kory-kyuh*
peas	peasair	*pe-siry*
porridge	lite/brochan	*lyi-chuh/bro-khan*
potato	buntàta	*bun taa-tuh*
salmon	bradan	*bra-tan*
sandwich	ceipire	*ke-piry-uh*
soup	brot	*brot*
toast	aran air a losgadh	*a-ran ery uh lo-skugh*
vegetables	glasraich	*glas-rikh*

Drinks

milk	bainne	*ba-nyuh*
(a cup of) coffee	(cupa) cofaidh	*(ku-puh) ko-fee*
(a cup of) tea	(cupa) tì	*(ku-puh) tee*
with milk	le bainne	*leh ba-nyuh*
without milk	gun bhainne	*gun va-nuh*
with sugar	le siùcar	*leh shoo-kary*
without sugar	gun siùcar	*gun shoo-kary*
orange juice	sùgh orains	*soo o-rinsh*
water	uisge	*ush-gyuh*

At the Pub

I'd like a ... of	bu toil leam ...	*bu tul lum ...*
glass	gloine	*glu-nyuh*
pint	pinnt	*peenj*
half-pint	leth phinnt	*leh feenj*
ale/lager	lionn	*lyoonn*
(red/white) wine	fìon (dearg/geal)	*fean (ja-rak/gyal)*
whisky	uisge-beatha	*ush-kyuh beh-huh*

It's my round.
'Se an turas agamsa
a tha ann.
*shey un tu-rus
a-kum-suh hown*

I'll get this one.
Gheobh mise am
fear/an té seo.
*yoe mee-shuh um
fer/un che sho*

SCOTTISH GAELIC

What will you have?
Dé ghabhas tu/sibh? (inf/pol) *je ghah-us doo/shiv?*

The same again.
An aon rud a-rithist. *un oon rut uh ree-ishch*

I've had enough, thanks.
Tha gu leòr agam, *ha guh lor a-kum*
tapadh leat/leibh. (inf/pol) *tah-puh laht/laiv*

| Cheers! | Slàinte mhór! | *slaan-chuh voer!* |
| | Slàinte mhath! | *slaan-chuh vah!* |

TIME, DATES & FESTIVALS

Monday	Di-Luain	*ji loo-any*
Tuesday	Di-Màirt	*ji maarshch*
Wednesday	Di-Ciadaoin	*ji kee-a-tany*
Thursday	Diar-daoin	*jur doony*
Friday	Di-hAoine	*ji hoo-nyuh*
Saturday	Di-Sathairne	*ji sa-hur-nuh*

There are two words used for Sunday – the first tends to be used by Catholics and Episcoplians, the second by Presbyterians.

| Sunday | Di-Domhnaich | *ji doe-nikh* |
| Sunday | Latha na Sàbaid | *lah-uh nuh saa-pach* |

Months

| January | am Faoilteach | *um fool-chakh* |
| February | an Gearran | *un gya-rran* |

SCOTTISH GAELIC

March	am Márt	*um maarsht*
April	an Giblean	*un gip-lun*
May	an Céitean	*un ke-chan*
June	an t-Ògmhìos	*un tok-vee-as*
July	an t-Iuchar	*un chu-khary*
August	an Lùnastal	*un loo-nu-stal*
September	an t-Sultain	*un tul-tiny*
October	an Damhair	*un da-vary*
November	an t-Samhain	*un tow-iny*
December	an Dubhlachd	*un doo-lakhk*

Festivals

an Nollaig
un no-laky
Christmas

a' Bhliadhna Ùr
uh vluh noor
New Year

Oidhche Shamhna
ai-khuh how-nuh
Hallowe'en

Latha Bealltainn
lah-huh byowl-tiny
May Day

Latha Lùnastail
lah-huh loo-nu-stal
Lammas Day

SCOTTISH GAELIC

Latha Fhéill Brighde
lah-huh ely bree-juh
first day of spring

Latha na Bliadhna Ùire
lah-huh nuh bluh noo-ryuh
New Year's Day

A' Chàisg
uh chaashk
Easter

Oidhche Challainn
aikh-uh cha-liny
Hogmanay; New Year's Eve
people normally visit friends and relatives after the New Year
has been rung in, exchanging drinks. This is commonly
referred to as 'first-footing'.

am Mòd
um mot
annual Gaelic arts festival, usually held in early October, with
a wide range of competitive music and theatre events

DID YOU KNOW ... The Celts used to count in
twenties and this ancient
way of counting is still used
in Gaelic and Welsh. The
decimal system shown here
has recently been devised
for use in schools, and is
taught alongside the older
'vigesimal' system.

NUMBERS

0	neoini	*nyo-nee*
1	a h-aon	*uh hoon*
2	a dhà	*uh ghaa*
3	a trì	*uh tree*
4	a ceithir	*uh ke-hiry*
5	a cóig	*uh coe-ik*
6	a sia	*uh shea*
7	a seachd	*uh shakhk*
8	a hochd	*uh hokhk*
9	a naoi	*uh nai*
10	a deich	*uh jekh*

To form the numbers 11 to 19, deug is added – deug being an old form of deich '10' (cf. English -teen and ten).

11	a h-aon deug	*uh hoon jeak*
12	a dhà dheug	*uh ghaa yeak*
13	a trì deug	*uh tree jeak*
14	a ceithir deug	*uh ke-hiry jeak*
15	a cóig deug	*uh koe-ik jeak*
16	a sia deug	*uh shea jeak*
17	a seachd deug	*uh shakhk jeak*
18	a h-ochd deug	*uh hokhk jeak*
19	a naoi deug	*a nai jeak*

SCOTTISH GAELIC

	Vigesimal	Decimal
20	fichead	fichead
30	deich ar fhichead	trithead
40	dá fhichead	ceathrad
50	dá fhichead is a deich	caogad/lethcheud
60	trí fichead	seasgad
70	trì fichead is a deich	seachdad
80	ceithir fichead	ochdad
90	ceithir fichead is a deich	naochad
100	ceud	ceud

Here are some more tricky numerals.

21	a h-aon ar fhichead
22	a dhà ar fhichead
33	a trì deug ar fhichead
44	dà fhichead is a ceithir
55	dá fhichead is cóig deug
66	trì fichead is a sia
77	trì fichead is a seachd deug
88	ceithir fichead is a h-ochd
99	ceithir fichead is a naoi deug

WELSH

INTRODUCTION

The Welsh language belongs to the Celtic branch of the Indo-European language family. Closely related to Breton and Cornish, and more distantly to Irish, Scottish and Manx, it is the strongest Celtic language both in terms of numbers of speakers (over 500,000) and place in society. It was once spoken throughout the island of Britain south of a line between modern Glasgow and Edinburgh, but was gradually pushed westwards by the invading Angles and Saxons following the retreat of the Roman legions in the 5th century. Several thousand Welsh speakers also live in the Welsh colony in Patagonia. Its earliest literature was written towards the end of the 6th century in what is now southern Scotland, when court poets Taliesin and Aneurin pioneered a literary tradition which continued for some 14 centuries.

By the early modern period, Welsh had lost its status as an official language. The Acts of Union with England (1536 and 1542) deprived the language of all administrative functions. However, translations of the Book of Common Prayer (1567) and the Bible (1588) into Welsh gave the language a limited public function again. Up until the industrial revolution, most Welsh people spoke only Welsh, and some 50% still spoke Welsh in 1900. Thereafter the language retreated more rapidly, so that by 1961, only 26% were Welsh-speaking and there was general alarm that the language would disappear.

The Saunders Lewis BBC radio lecture, Tynged yr Iaith *tuhng-ed uhrr yaith*, 'The Fate of the Language' in 1962 led to the creation of Cymdeithas yr Iaith Gymraeg *kuhm-day-thas uhrr yaith guhm-raig*, a protest movement in support of the language. It was spearheaded by university students and inspired by pop singers like Dafydd Iwan, and succeeded through campaigns of civil disobedience in winning equal recognition for Welsh in one domain of society after another. Recent figures would suggest that the decline has been halted. The language has reasserted its position in the educational system, with the Welsh-language TV channel S4C since 1983, and in recent years with the resurgence of Welsh as a badge of national identity, particularly among the young.

PRONUNCIATION

Transliterations have been provided in this chapter as an additional guide to pronunciation (see page 231 for guide to transliterations). All letters in Welsh are pronounced and the stress is usually on the second last syllable. Letters are pronounced as in English except for:

Vowels

a short as the 'a' in 'map';
   long as the 'a' in 'margin'
e short as the 'e' in 'pen';
   long as the 'ea' in 'pear'
i short as the 'i' in 'bit';
   long as the 'ea' in 'beat'
o short as the 'o' in 'box';
   long as 'o' in 'bore'
u as i (short and long)
w short as the 'oo' in 'book';
   long as the 'oo' in 'spook'
y as i (short or long);
   sometimes like the 'a' in 'about', especially in
   common one-syllable words like y, yr, fy, dy and yn

Vowels can be long or short. Those marked with a circumflex (^) are always long and those with a grave accent ( ) short.

In words of one syllable, vowels which are followed by two consonants (remember that ch, dd, ff, ng, ll, ph, rh, and th count as single consonants in Welsh) are short such as corff 'body'. If a monosyllabic word ends in p, t, c, m, or ng, the vowel is short such as llong 'ship'. If it ends in b, d, g, f, dd, ff, th, ch, or s, the vowel is long such as in bad 'boat', as is any vowel ending a one-syllable word, such as pla 'plague'.

In words of more than one syllable, all unstressed vowels are short, such as in the first and final vowels of cariadon 'lovers'. Stressed vowels can be long or short and in general follow the rules for vowels in monosyllables.

Diphthongs

ae/ai/au	as the 'y' in 'my'
aw	as the 'ow' in 'cow'
ei/eu/ey	as the 'ay' in 'day'
ew	as short 'e' followed by 'oo'
iw/uw/yw	as the 'ew' in 'few'
oe/oi	as 'oy' in 'boy'
ow	as the 'ow' in 'tow'
wy	sometimes as 'uey' as in 'chop suey'; sometimes like the 'wi' in 'window' (especially after 'g')

Consonants

c	always as 'k'
ch	as the 'ch' in Scottish 'loch'
dd	as the 'th' in 'this'
ff	as the 'f' in 'fork'
g	always as the 'g' in 'garden', not as in 'gentle'
ng	as the 'ng' in 'sing'
ll	as 'hl' (put the tongue in the position for 'l' and breathe out)
ph	as 'f'
r	rolled as in Spanish
rh	pronounced as 'hr'
s	always as the 's' in 'say', never as the 's' in 'busy'
si	as the 'sh' in 'shop'
th	always as the 'th' in 'thin'

Sound Changes

Sometimes the initial consonant of a word changes its sound to convey grammatical meaning. The consonant may change to become softer, nasal or aspirated.

Initial consonant	Soft	Nasal	Aspirated
p	b	mh	ph
t	d	nh	th
c	g	ngh	ch
b	f	m	
d	dd	n	
g		ng	
ll	l		
m	f		
rh	r		

WELSH

GRAMMAR
Word Order

The usual word order in Welsh, as in other Celtic languages but unlike most European languages, is verb-subject-object.

The girl bought a pint.   Prynodd y ferch beint.
                            (lit: bought the girl pint)

Articles

Welsh has no indefinite article corresponding to 'a' or 'an'. The definite article has three forms:

y before a consonant
  y ffarmwr   *uh farm-oorr*   the farmer

yr before a vowel and 'h'
  yr oen   *uhrr oyn*   the lamb

r after a vowel
  y ffarmwr a'r oen *uh farm-oorr arr oyn* the farmer
                                             and the lamb

Nouns

Nouns can be masculine or feminine, plural or singular. The initial consonant of feminine nouns changes to a 'soft' sound after the definite article.

| merch | *merkh* | a girl |
| y ferch | *uh verkh* | the girl |

Plurals

The plural may be formed in several ways:

Adding plural suffixes such as -au

| afal | *av-al* | apple |
| afalau | *av-al-ai* | apples |

Internal changes

| car | *kahr* | a car |
| ceir | *kayrr* | cars |

A mixture of both

| gwraig | *gwraig* | wife |
| gwragedd | *gwrag-eth* | wives |

WELSH

NICKNAMES

The Welsh have a fondness for nicknames. Beti Byngalo *bet-tee buhn-ga-loh* 'Betty Bungalow' is so named because she hasn't got much upstairs (she's stupid) and Huw Goc Aur *hugh gok airr* 'Huw Golden Cock' for reasons easily imagined.

WELSH

Adjectives

Adjectives generally follow the noun they modify.

ci mawr	*kee mowrr*	dog big
		'a big dog'

Some adjectives have plural and feminine forms.

melyn	*mel-in*	yellow (m sg)
melen	*mel-en*	(f sg)
melynion	*mel-**uhn**-nyon*	(pl m & f)

Phrases that equate one thing with another are formed by adding the suffix -ed:

coch	*kohkh*	red
coched	***kohk**-ed*	as red

Or by using of mor + adjective for words of more than one syllable.

mor ddiddorol	*morr dhi-**thor**-ol*	as interesting

The comparative can be formed by either:

adding the suffix -ach

del	*del*	pretty
delach	***del**-akh*	prettier

or by using mwy + adjective

mwy arwyddocaol	*muey arr-**with**-ok-ah-ol*	more significant

The superlative can be formed by adding the suffix -af

hyll	*hihl*	ugly
hyllaf	***huh**-hlav*	ugliest

or by using mwyaf + adjective

mwyaf cerddorol	***muey**-av-kerr-**thorr**-ol*	most musical

INDEPENDENT PRONOUNS

I	mi/fi	*mee/vee*
you	ti/di (sg inf)	*tee/dee*
	chi (sg pol)	
he	ef	*ehv*
she	hi	*hee*
we	ni	*nee*
you	chi (pl)	*khee*
they	nhw	*noo*

WELSH

DEPENDENT PRONOUNS

	Prefixed	Infixed	Affixed
I	fy *vuh*	'm *m*	i/fi *ee/vee*
you	dy *duh*	'th *th*	di/ti *dee/tee*
he	ei *ee*	'i/'w *ee/w*	ef/fo/fe *ehv/voh/veh*
she	ei *ee*	'i/'w *ee/w*	hi *hee*
we	ein *uhn*	'n *n*	ni *nee*
you	eich *uhkh*	'ch *kh*	chi *khee*
they	eu *ee*	'u/'w *ee/w*	nhw *noo*

Demonstratives

this	hwn (m)	this one	hwn (m)
	hoon		
	hon (f)		hon (f)
	hon		*hon*
	hyn (abstract)		
	hin		
these	hyn	these ones	rhain
	hin		*hrain*
that	hwnnw (m)	that one	hwnna (m)
	hoon-noo		*hon-na*
	honno (f)		honna (f)
	hon-no		*hon-na*
	hynny (abstract)		
	huhn-nee		
those	hynny	those ones	rheini
	huhn-nee		*hray-nee*

WELSH

Yma *uh-ma* 'here' and yna *uh-na* 'there' are also commonly used with the definite article as demonstrative adjectives.

| y ty yma | *uh tee uh-ma* | this house |
| y bechgyn yna | *uh bekh-gin uh-na* | those boys |

Verbs
To Have

The verb 'to have' has two forms in Welsh. One form is mainly used in northern Wales (north of Aberystwyth).

Mae gen i gar.   *mai gen ee gar*   I have a car.

The second is used in the south. In the southern form, the possessed object appears within, and not at the end of, the phrase.

Northern Forms of 'To Have'

I have	mae gen i	mai gen ee
you have	mae gen ti	mai gen tee
he has	mae ganddo fo/fe	mai gan-tho voh/veh
she has	mae ganddi hi	mai gan-thee hee
we have	mae gynnon ni	mai guhn-non nee
you have	mae gynnokh khi	mai guhn-nokh khee
they have	mae ganddyn nhw	mai gan-thin noo

Southern Forms of 'To Have'

I have	mae ... gyda fi	mai ... guh-da vee
you have	mae ... gyda ti	mai ... guh-da tee
he has	mae ... gydag e	mai ... guh-dag e
she has	mae ... gyda hi	mai ... guh-da hee
we have	mae ... gyda ni	mai ... guh-da nee
you have	mae ... gyda chi	mai ... guh-da khee
they have	mae ... gyda nhw	mai ... guh-da noo

WELSH

To Be (Present)

I am	dw i	doo-wee
you are	rwyt ti	rrueyt tee
he is	mae e	mai e
she is	mae hi	mai hee
we are	rydyn ni	rruh-din nee
you are	rydych chi	rruh-deekh khee
they are	maen nhw	mighn noo

WELSH

To Be (Past)

I was	roeddwn i	*rroy-thoon ee*
you were	roeddet ti	*rroy-thet tee*
he was	roedd e	*rroyth e*
she was	roedd hi	*rroyth hee*
we were	roedden ni	*rroy-then nee*
you were	roeddech chi	*rroy-thek khee*
they were	roedden nhw	*rroy-then noo*

Prepositions

Prepositions can be uninflected, or inflected according to person.

ar	*arr*	on
mae'r ci ar y bwrdd	*mairr kee arr uh boorth*	The dog is on the table.
mae'r ci arno	*mairr kee arr-no*	The dog is on it.

Inflected Forms of 'On'

arna i	*arr-na ee*	on me
arnat ti	*arr-nat tee*	on you
arno ef	*arr-no ehv*	on him/it
arni hi	*arr-nee hee*	on her/it
arnon ni	*arr-non nee*	on us
arnoch chi	*arr-nokh khee*	on you
arnyn nhw	*arr-nin noo*	on the

MEETING PEOPLE
You Should Know

Hello.
   Sut mae.   *sit mai*

Goodbye.
   Hwyl fawr.   *hueyl vowrr*

Excuse me.
   Esgusodwch fi.   *ess-gi-so-dookh vee*

May I?
   Ga i?   *gah ee?*

Do you mind?
   Oes ots gyda chi?   *oys ots guh-da khee?*

Sorry (excuse me; forgive me).
   Mae'n ddrwg gyda fi.   *main thrroog guh-da vee*

Please.
   Os gwelwch in dda.   *os gwel-ookh uhn thah*

Thank you (very much).
   Diolch (in fawr iawn). *dee-olkh (uhn vowrr yown)*

You're welcome.
   Croeso.   *kroy-ssoh*

Don't mention it.
   Peidiwch â sôn.   *payd-yookh ah sohn*

I don't know.
   Wn i ddim.   *oon ee thim*

Yes/No
   oes/nac oes   *oyss/nag oyss*

Greetings & Goodbyes

Good morning.
   Bore da.   *bo-rre dah*

Good afternoon.
   Prynhawn da.   *pruhn-hown dah*

WELSH

WELSH

Good evening.
  Noswaith dda. *noss-waith thah*

Goodnight.
  Nos da. *nohs dah*

See you (later).
  Wela i chi (wedyn). *wel-ah ee khee (we-din)*

CONGRATULATIONS!

Happy Birthday!
  Pen Blwydd Hapus! *pen blueyth hah-piss!*
Happy Christmas!
  Nadolig Llawen! *nah-doll-ig hlow-en!*
Happy New Year!
  Blwyddyn Newydd Dda! *bluey-thin ne-with thah!*
Congratulations!
  Llongyfarchiadau! *hlon-guh-vahr-khyad-ai!*
Cheers!
  Iechyd Da! *yekh-id dah!*
Get well soon!
  Brysiwch wella! *bruhsh-ookh we-hlah!*
Bless you! (when sneezing)
  Bendith! *ben-dith!*
What a pity!
  Dyna drueni! *duh-nah dree-en-ee!*
Bon voyage!
  Siwrnai dda! *shoorr-neh thah!*
Good luck!
  Pob lwc! *pohb look!*
Hope it goes well!
  Pob hwyl! *pohb hueyl!*

How are you?
   Sut ydych chi?   *sit uh-deekh khee?*

(Very) well.
   (Da) iawn.   *(dah) yown*

First Encounters

What's your name?
   Beth yw eich enw chi?   *beth yu uhch en-oo khee?*

My name's ...
   Fy enw i yw ...   *ne-noo ee yu ...*

I'd like to introduce you to ...
   Ga i gyflwyno ... i chi.   *gah ee guh-vluey-noh ... ee khee*

Pleased to meet you.
   Mae'n dda gen i gwrdd   *mighn thah gen ee goorrth*
   â chi.   *ah khee*

Where do you live?
   Ble ydych chi'n byw?   *bleh uh-deekh kheen byoo?*

I live in (Darwin).
   Dw i'n byw in (Darwin).   *doo een byoo uhn (Darwin)*

I'm here ...   Dw i yma ...   *doo ee uh-mah ...*

   on business   ar fusnes   *arr viss-ness*

   on holiday   ar wyliau   *arr wil-yai*

   studying   yn astudio   *uhn ah-stid-yoh*

Nationalities

Where are you from?
   O ble ydych chi'n dod?   *oh ble uh-deekh kheen dohd?*

I'm from ...   Dw i'n dod o ...   *doo een dohd oh ...*

   Australia   Awstralia   *ow-strra-lee-ah*

WELSH

WELSH

Canada	Ganada	*gah-nah-dah*
England	Loegr	*loy-gerr*
Ireland	Iwerddon	*ee-werr-thon*

New Zealand	Seland Newydd	*se-land neh-with*
Scotland	Yr Alban	*uhrr al-ban*
the USA	Yr Unol	*uhrr in-ol dah-lay-*
	Daleithiau	*thee-ai*

Occupations

What do you do?

	Beth ydych chi'n wneud?	*beth uh-deekh kheen nayd?*
I'm (a/an) ...	Dw i'n ...	*doo een ...*
artist	arlunydd	*arr-lin-ith*
business person	berson busnes	*ber-sson biss-ness*
doctor	feddyg	*veth-ig*
engineer	beiriannydd	*bayrr-yan-eeth*
journalist	newyddiadurwr (m)	*ne-with-yad-*
		dirr-oorr
	newyddiadurwraig (f)	*ne-with-ya-dirr-raig*

lawyer	gyfreithwraig (f)	*guh-vrrayth-rreyeg*
	gyfreithiwr (m)	*guh-vrayth-yoorr*
musician	gerddor	*gerr-thorr*
nurse	nyrs	*nurrse*
office worker	gweithio mewn	*gway-thyo meh-oon*
	swyddfa	*sueyth-vah*
scientist	wyddonydd	*wi-thon-eeth*
secretary	ysgrifenyddes (f)	*uh-sgrree-ven-uhth-ess*
	ysgrifennydd (m)	*uhsgrree-ven-eeth*
teacher	athrawes (f)	*ah-thrrow-ess*
	athro (m)	*ah-thrroh*
waiter	weinydd	*wayn-eeth*

I'm ...	Dw I ...	*doo ee ...*
retired	wedi ymddeol	*we-dee uhm-theh-ol*
unemployed	y n ddi-waith	*uhn thee waith*

WELSH

GRAFFITI

Dim ...	No ...
Na i ...	No to ...
Cymru Rydd!	Free Wales!
Nid yw Cymru ar Werth	Wales is Not for Sale
Dim Tai Newydd	No New Houses
Cofiwch Dryweryn	Remember Tryweryn (the village flooded to make a reservoir to provide water for England)

WELSH

Family

Do you have a partner?
> Oes partner gennych chi?   *oyss **parrt-nerr** gen-eekh khee?*

Do you have a girlfriend/boyfriend?
> Oes cariad gennych chi?   *oyss **karr-yad** gen-eekh khee?*

How many children do you have?
> Faint o blant sy gennych   *vaint oh **blant** see gen-eekh*
> chi?   *khee?*

I'm ...	Dw i'n ...	*doo een ...*
gay; a lesbian	hoyw; lesbiad	*hoy-yoo; less-bee-yad*
married	briod	*brree-od*
separated	dw i wedi gwahanu	*doo ee we-dee*
		gwa-han-ee
single	sengl	*seng-el*
a widow/	wraig weddw/r	*urraig **weth**-oo/oorr*
widower	gweddw	***gweth**-oo*

Language Difficulties

I speak a little Welsh.
> Dw i'n siarad tipyn bach   *doo ee'n sharr-ad ti-pin bahkh*
> o Gymraeg.   *oh guhm-raig*

I don't understand.
> Dw i ddim in deall.   *doo ee **thim** uhn deh-ahhl*

Could you speak more slowly please?
> Allwch chi siarad in arafach,   *ahl-ookh khee sharr-ad uhn arr-*
> os gwelwch in dda?   *av-akh, os gwel-ookh uhn **thah**?*

Could you repeat that?
> Allwch chi ddweud hynny   *ahl-ookh khee **thwayd** huh-nee*
> eto?   *eh-toh?*

Could you write that down please?
Allwch chi sgrifennu hynny   *ahl-ookh khee sgri-ven-nee huh-*
i lawr, os gwelwch in dda?   *nee ee lowrr, os gwel-ookh*
                             uhn thah?

How do you say ...?
Sut mae dweud ...?   *sit mai dwayd ...?*

What's this called in Welsh?
Beth yw hwn in Gymraeg?   *beth yu hoon uhn guhm-raig?*

Interests

What do you like doing?
Beth ydych chi'n hoffi   *beth uh-deekh kheen hof-ee*
wneued?   *nayd?*

I like swimming and going to the cinema.
Dw i'n hoffi nofio a mynd   *doo een hof-ee nov-yoh ah*
i'r sinema.   *mind eerr sin-em-ah*

I don't like cooking.
Dw i ddim in hoffi   *doo ee thim uhn hof-ee*
coginio.   *koh-gin-yo*

What do you do in your spare time?
Beth ydych chi'n wneud   *beth uh-deekh kheen nayd uhn*
in eich amser hamdden?   *uhkh am-sserr ham-then?*

I play chess.
Dw i'n chwarae   *doo een khwarr-eh*
gwyddbwyll.   *gueyth-bueyhl*

Do you like sport?
Ydych chi'n hoffi   *uh-deekh kheen hof-ee*
chwaraeon?   *khwa-ray-on?*

Yes, very much.
Ydw, in fawr iawn. *uh-doo, uhn vowrr yown*

No, not at all.
Nac ydw, dim o gwbl. *nag uh-doo, **dim** oh goo-bool*

GOING OUT

What are you doing this evening?
Beth ydych chi'n wneud *beth uh-deekh kheen **nayd***
heno? *hen-oh?*

Nothing special.
Dim byd arbennig. *dim beed arr-**ben**-ig*

Would you like to go out somewhere?
Hoffech chi fynd allan *hof-ekh khee vind **ahl**-an ee*
i rywle? *rree-oo-leh?*

Would you like to go for a drink/meal?
Hoffech chi fynd allan am *hof-ekh khee vind **ahl**-an am*
ddiod/bryd o fwyd? *<u>th</u>ee-od/brreed oh **vueyd**?*

I'll buy.
Fe dala i. *veh **dah**-lah ee*

Do you feel like (going for a swim)?
Oes awydd (mynd i nofio) *oyss **ow**-wi<u>th</u> (mind ee nov-yoh)*
arnoch chi? *arrn-okh khee?*

Yes, where to?
Hoffwn. Ble awn ni? *hof-oon bleh **own** nee?*

Yes, that'd be great.
Oes, byddai hynny'n wych. *oyss, buh-dheh **huh**-neen weekh*

Yes, that'd be lovely.
Hoffwn, byddai hynny'n *hof-oon, buh-<u>th</u>eh **huh**-neen*
hyfryd. *huh-vrrid*

OK.
    Iawn.   *iown*

No, I'm afraid I can't.
    Alla i ddim mae arna i ofn.   *ahl-ah ee <u>th</u>im mai **arrn**-ah ee*
                                  ov-on

I'm sorry, I can't.
    Mae'n ddrwg gen i, alla   *main <u>th</u>roog gen ee, ahl-ah ee*
    i ddim.   *<u>th</u>im*

Not at the moment, thanks.
    Ddim ar hyn o bryd,   *dhim arr hin oh brreed, dee-olkh*
    diolch.

INSULTS

Shut your mouth!	Cau dy geg! *kye duh gehg!*
Piss off!	Cer i grafu! *ker ee grah-vee!*
Fuck you!	Twll dy din di (ffaro)! *toolh duh deen dee (fah-ro)!*
Go to hell!	Cer i'r diawl! *ker eer jowl!*
Creep!	Y Sbrych! *uh sbreekh!*
Idiot!	Y Twpsyn! *uh toop-ssin!*
You old devil!	Yr hen ddiawl i ti! *uhrr hen <u>th</u>yowl ee tee!*
You scheming bastard!	Y sinach dan din i ti! *uh shee-nach dan deen ee tee!*

WELSH

What about tomorrow?
Beth am yfory? *beth am uh-vorr-ee?*

I feel like going to ...
Mae gen i awydd mynd I ... *mai gen ee ow-eeth mind ee ...*

Arranging to Meet

What time shall we meet?
Am faint o'r gloch wnawn *am vaint ohrr glokh wnown*
ni gyfarfod? *nee guh-vahr-vod?*

Where shall we meet?
Ble wnawn ni gyfarfod? *bleh wnown nee guh-vahr-vod?*

UNIQUE WELSH EXPRESSIONS

Bydda i 'na 'na. *buh-<u>th</u>ah ee nah nowrr*
I'll be there sometime in the future.
(lit: I'll be there now)

cerdd dant *ker<u>th</u> dant*
strict-metre poetry sung in counterpoint to a tune
on the harp
(lit: string music)

cynghanedd *kuhng-han-e<u>th</u>*
system of consonance or alliteration in a line of
strict-metre Welsh poetry

eisteddfod *ayss-te<u>th</u>-vod*
competitive arts festival

hiraeth *heerr-aith*
grief or sadness after the loss of something or
someone

hwyl *hueyl*
well-being/fervour/gusto/fun

Let's meet at (eight o'clock) in St Mary Street.

Beth am gyfarfod am (wyth o'r gloch) yn Heol y Santes Fair.

beth am guh-vahrr-vod am (ueyth ohr glokh) uhn heh-ool uh sant-ess vairr

OK. I'll see you then.

Iawn. Wela i chi bryd hynny.

yown we-lah ee khee brreed hu-hnee

Afterwards

It was nice talking to you.

Roedd hi'n braf siarad â chi.

royth heen brrahv sha-rrad ah khee

I have to get going now.

Rhaid imi fynd nawr.

hraid i-mee vind nowrr

I had a great day/evening.

Ces i ddiwrnod gwych/noson wych.

kehss ee thee-oorr-nod gweekh/noss-on weekh

Hope to see you again soon.

Gobeithio eich gweld chi eto in fuan.

go-bay-thyo uhkh gweld khee eh-toh uhn vee-an

I'll give you a call.

Ffônia i chi.

foh-nyah ee khee

What's your number?

Beth yw eich rhif?

beth yu uhkh hrreev?

FOOD & DRINK
Eating Out

Table for ... please.

Bwrdd i ... os gwelwch in dda.

boorrdh ee ... oss gwel-ookh uhn thah

Can I see the menu please?
Ga i weld y fwydlen, os   *gah ee weld uh vueyd-len, oss*
gwelwch in dda?   *gwel-ookh uhn <u>thah</u>?*

The bill, please.
Y bil, os gwelwch in dda.   *uh bill, oss gwel-ookh uhn <u>thah</u>*

Traditional Welsh Dishes

bara brith   *bah-ra breeth*
rich, fruited tea-loaf

bara lawr   *bah-ra lowrr*
laver seaweed boiled and mixed with oatmeal and
traditionally served with bacon for breakfast

cawl   *cowl*

broth of meat and vegetables

caws caerffili   *cows kairr-fil-ee*
Caerphilly cheese, a crumbly salty cheese that used to be
popular with miners

ffagots a pys   *fa-gots a peess*

seasoned balls of chopped pork and liver in gravy served
with peas

lobsgows   *lobs-gowss*

a Northwalian version of cawl

pice ar y maen   *pi-keh ar uh mahn*
(lit: cakes on the griddlestone) Small, fruited scone-like
griddle cakes known also as Welsh cakes

In the Pub

I'd like a (half) pint of ...	Ga i (hanner o) beint o ...	*gah ee (hann-err oh) baynt oh ...*
bitter	chwerw	*khwe-rroo*
cider	seidr	*say-dirr*
lager	lager	*la-gerr*
orange juice	sudd oren	*seeth oh-ren*
water	dwr	*doorr*

WELSH

PLACENAMES

The Welsh and English names of a town can be quite different.

Swansea	Abertawe	*ab-er-tow-eh*
Newport	Casnewydd	*kass-ne-with*
Holyhead	Caergybi	*kairr-guh-bee*

Some can be a mouthful, such as the (in)famous town called

Llanfairpwllgwyngyllgogerychwyrndrobwllllantysiliogogogoch
*hlan-vairr-poohl-gwin-gihl-go-gerr-uh-khwirrn-dro-
boohl-hlan-tuh-sil-ee-oh-go-go-gokh*

while others are comparatively simple, such as Splott *splot*, Mwnt
moont and Plwm *ploomp*.

Place names are often built on words that describe a feature of the countryside.

aber	*ab-berr*	estuary/confluence
afon	*a-von*	river
bach	*bahkh*	small
bro	*broh*	vale
bryn	*brin*	hill
caer	*kairr*	fort
cwm	*koom*	valley
dinas	*dee-nass*	hill fortress
eglwys	*eglueyss*	church
fach	*vahkh*	small
fawr	*vowrr*	big
isa (f)	*issa*	lower
llan	*hlan*	church/enclosure
llyn	*hlin*	lake
maes	*maiss*	field
mawr	*mowrr*	big
mynydd	*muhnee__th__*	mountain
pen	*pen*	head/top/end
uchaf	*ikhav*	upper
ynys	*uh-niss*	island/holm/ watermeadow

WELSH

TIME, DATES & FESTIVALS
Days

Monday	dydd Llun	*dee__th__ hleen*
Tuesday	dydd Mawrth	*dee__th__ mowrrth*
Wednesday	dydd Mercher	*dee__th__ merr-kherr*
Thursday	dydd Iau	*dee__th__ yigh*
Friday	dydd Gwener	*dee__th__ gwen-err*
Saturday	dydd Sadwrn	*dee__th__ sad-oorrn*
Sunday	dydd Sul	*dee__th__ seel*

Months

Some names for months are borrowed from Latin. Others are native Welsh.

January	Ionawr	*yon-owrr*
February	Chwefror	*khwe-vrrohrr*
March	Mawrth	*mowrrth*
April	Ebrill	*eh-brihl*
May	Mai	*mai*
June	Mehefin	*me-he-vin*
	(lit: the middle of summer)	
July	Gorffennaf	*gor-fen-ahv*
	(lit: the end of summer)	
August	Awst	*owst*
September	Medi	*med-dee*
	(lit: reaping)	
October	Hydref	*huh-drev*
	(the rutting season, lit: stag-roaring)	
November	Tachwedd	*Tahkh-weth*
	(the time for slaughtering animals before winter, lit: slaughter)	
December	Rhagfyr	*hrag-virr*
	(the shortest day, lit: before short)	

Festivals

Dydd Calan   *deeth ka-lan*

New Year's Day. Traditionally, children would go from house-to-house singing special new year songs and asking for a gift.

WELSH

Santes Dwynwen   *sant-ess **dueyn-wen***
   St Dwynwen is the Welsh patron saint of lovers and her
   feast-day is on 25 January

Dydd Gwyl Dewi   *deeth gueyl **de-wee***
   St David's Day, 1 March. St David is the patron saint
   of Wales.

Eisteddfod Genedlaethol   *ay-steth-vod gen-ed-lay-thol*
   competitive arts festival held in the first week of August

NUMBERS

0	dim	*dim*
1	un	*een*
2	dau/dwy (f)	*dy/duey* (f)
3	tri/tair (f)	*tree/tairr*
4	pedwar/pedair (f)	*ped-wahrr /ped-airr*
5	pump	*pimp*
6	chwech	*khwekh*
7	saith	*saith*
8	wyth	*ueyth*
9	naw	*now*
10	deg	*dehg*

The Celts used to count in twenties and this ancient way of counting is still used in Welsh and Gaelic today. This system, known as the 'vegisimal' system, is also used by the French, who inherited it from the Gauls. The decimal system is given in the right hand column.

THE WELSH WEEK

The Celts used to measure time in nights rather than days. The Welsh word for week is wythnos *ueyth-noss* (lit: eight nights) and a fortnight is pythefnos *puh-thev-noss* (lit: 15 nights).

	Vegisimal system	**Decimal system**
11	unarddeg *een-ahrr-thehg*	un deg un *een dehg-een*
12	deuddeg *day-thehg*	un deg dau *een dehg dai*
13	tri ar ddeg *tree-ahrr-thehg*	un deg tri *een dehg tree*
14	pedwar ar ddeg *ped-wahrr-ahr-thehg*	un deg pedwar *een dehg ped-wahrr*
15	pymtheg *puhm-thehg*	un deg pump *een dehg pimp*
16	un ar bymtheg *een-ahrr-buhmthehg*	un deg chwech *een dehg khwekh*
17	dau ar bymtheg *dai-ahrr-buhmthehg*	un deg saith *een dehg saith*
18	deunaw *day-now*	un deg wyth *een dehg ueyth*
19	pedwar ar bymtheg *fed-wahrr-ahrr-buhmthehg*	un deg naw *een dehg now*
20	ugain *ig-ain*	dau ddeg *dai thehg*
21	un ar hugain *een-ahrr-hig-ain*	dau ddeg un *dai thehg een*
22	dau ar hugain *dai-ahrr-hig-ain*	dau ddeg dau *dai thehg dai*
23	tri ar hugain *trree-ahrr-hig-ain*	dau ddeg tri *dai thehg tree*
30	deg ar hugain *dehg-ahrr-hig-ain*	tri deg *tree dehg*
40	deugain *day-gain*	pedwar deg *ped-wahrr dehg*

WELSH

WELSH

ORDINAL NUMBERS

1st	cyntaf	*kuhn-tahv*
2nd	ail	*ail*
3rd	trydydd	*truh-dee<u>th</u>*

50	hannar cant	pump deg	
	hann-err kant	*pimp dehg*	
60	trigain	chwech deg	
	tri-gain	*khwekh degh*	
70	deg a thrigain	saith deg	
	dehg-ah-thrri-gain	*saith dehg*	
80	pedwar ugain	wyth deg	
	ped-wahrr ig-ain	*ueyth degh*	
90	deg a phedwar ugain	naw deg	
	dehg-ah-fed-wahrr ig-ain	*now dehg*	
99	pedwar ar bymthgeg	naw deg naw	
	ped-wahrr ahrr buhm-thehg	*now dehg now*	
	a phedwar ugain		
	a phed-wahrr ig-ain		
100	cant	*kant*	
1000	mil	*meel*	

Suggested Reading

SUGGESTED READING

General

Bryson, B. 1991, *The Mother Tongue: English and How it Got That Way*, Penguin

Bryson, B. 1997, *Notes from a Small Island*, Avon Press

Burchfield, R. 1981, *The Spoken Word: A BBC Guide*, British Broadcasting Corporation

Burchfield, R. 1985, *The English Language*, Oxford University Press

Burgen, S. 1997, *Your Mother's Tongue*, Victor Gollanz

Crowe, R. (ongoing), *Dictionary of the Welsh Language*, University of Wales

Crystal, D. 1988, *The English Language*, Penguin

Crystal, D. 1995, *The Cambridge Encyclopaedia of the English Language*, Cambridge University Press

Foster, B. 1981, *The Changing English Language*, Macmillan

Honey, J. 1989, *Does Accent Matter?: the Pygmalion Factor*, Faber

Jennings, C. 1995, *Up North: Travels Beyond the Watford Gap*, Abacus

Leith, D. 1997, *A Social History of English*, Routledge

McArthur, T. 1992, *The Oxford Companion to the English Language*, Oxford University Press

McCrum, R., W. Cran & R. MacNeil 1986, *The Story of English*, Faber & Faber

Trudgill, P. 1984, *Language in the British Isles*, Cambridge University Press

Trudgill, P. 1990, *The Dialects of England*, Blackwell

Upton, C. & J. Widdowson 1996, *An Atlas of English Dialects*, Oxford University Press

By Region

Coggle, P. 1993, *Do You Speak Estuary? The New Standard English*, Bloomsbury Press

Dobson, S. 1987, *Larn Yersel' Geordie*, Butler Press

Downes, J. 1986, *A Dictionary of Devon Dialect*, Tabb House

Graham, F. 1987, *The New Geordie Dictionary*, Butler Press

Johnson, E. 1990, *Yorkshire – English*, Abson Books

Jones, J. 1991, *Rhyming Cockney Slang*, Abson Books

Kay, B. 1993, *Scots: the Mither Tongue* (second edition), Alloway Publishing

McClure, J. 1997, *Why Scots Matters*, The Saltire Society

Ó Maolalaigh, R. with I. MacAonghuis 1996, *Scottish Gaelic in Three Months*, Dorling Kindersley (formerly published by Hugo Language Books)

Thompson, D (ed.) 1994, *The Companion to Gaelic Scotland*, Gairm Publications

Todd, G. 1987, *Todd's Geordie Words and Phrases: an Aid to Communication on Tyneside and Thereabouts*, Butler Press

Warrack, A. 1988, *The Scots Dialect Dictionary*, Lomond Press

Wright, P. 1981, *Cockney Dialect and Slang*, Batsford

Wright, P. 1986, *The Yorkshire Yammer: How it is Spoke*, Dalesman Press

Wright, P. 1989, *Cumbrian Chat: How it is Spoke*, Dalesman Press

Academic

Ball, M. (ed.) 1993, *The Celtic Languages*, Routledge

Bauer, L. 1994, *Watching English Change: an Introduction to the Study of Linguistic Change in Standard Englishes in the Twentieth Century*, Longman

Brook, G. 1963, *English Accents*, André Deutsch

Coupland, N. 1988, *Dialect in Use: Sociolinguistic Variation in Cardiff English*, University of Wales Press

Foulkes, P. & G. Docherty (forthcoming, eds.) *Urban Voices*, E.J. Arnold

Gimson, A. 1994, revised by A. Cruttenden. *Gimson's Pronunciation of English*, fifth edition, E.J. Arnold

Hughes, A. & P. Trudgill 1996, *English Accents and Dialects: an Introduction to Social and Regional Varieties of English in the British Isles*, Arnold

Knowles, G. 1974, *Scouse: the Urban Dialect of Liverpool*, PhD thesis, University of Leeds

MacAulay, D. (ed.) 1992, *The Celtic Languages*, Cambridge University Press

MacKinnon, K. 1991, *Gaelic: A Past and Future Prospect*, Saltire

Milroy, L. & J. Milroy (eds) 1993, *Real English: the Grammar of English Dialects in the British Isles*, Longman

North, D. 1986, *Studies in Anglo-Cornish: Aspects of the History and Geography of English Pronunciation in Cornwall*, Institute of Cornish Studies

O'Donnell, W. & L. Todd 1991, *Variety in Contemporary English*, second edition, Harper Collins

Orton, H. & E. Dieth 1962-68, *The Survey of English Dialects*, E.J. Arnold

Parry, D. 1977, *The Survey of Anglo-Welsh Dialects*, vol. 1, University College Swansea Press

Wakelin, M. 1972, *English dialects: an introduction*, Athlone Press

Wells, J. 1982, *Accents of English*, Cambridge University Press

Withers, C. 1984, *Gaelic in Scotland 1698–1981: The Geographical History of a Language*, John Donald Publishers

MAPS

London and the South-East ... 186
North-East England 194
North-West England 207
Scotland 200
South-West England.............. 219
Wales 212
West Midlands 215
Yorkshire 190

TEXT

BRITISH ENGLISH 11

Abbreviations 34, 179
Accents 183
  Estuary English 188
  London 186
  North-East England 194
  North-West England 207
  Posh English 187
  Scotland 199
  South-East England 186
  South-West England 219
  Wales 212
  West Midlands 215
  Yorkshire 189
Accommodation 79
Acronyms 179
American – British 159
  Ambiguous Terms 177
  British Words 164
  Differences in Phrasing 163
  Spelling 159
  Suffixes 159
  Phrases 161
  Words 160
Around Town 83
Beer 104, 108-110
Borrowing 19
Brand Names 62

Children 46
Clothes 114
Cockney 65
Common Expressions 55
Cornish 62
Cricket 138
  Chants 142
  Grounds 141
  Rules 139
  Stars 140

Dialects .... (see Accents)
Drinks 103
Drugs 59
Drunkenness 227

Education 152
English, 'Good' 28
  Spread of 31
Entertainment 111
Estuary English 30, 188
Expressions 49

Festivals 121
Fleet Street 85
Food 95
Football 125
  Annual Events 130
  Chants 125

England's Team 130
Football League 128
Major Teams 129
Positions 128
Scotland's Team 132
Scottish League 129
Wales' Team 132
French Influence 16

Games 143
Gender 23
Getting Around 71
Bicycle 78
Buses 73
Car 74
Taxi 73
Trains 71
Government & Politics 147
Greetings 43

Highland Games 113
History 11
House, Around the 81
Housing 80

In the Country 91
Introduction 11
Invasions 15

Letterboxing 93

Markets, London 112
Meeting People 43
Metaphor 21
Morris Dancing 115
Music 119

Newspapers
Fleet Street 85
Tabloids 18
Norman Conquest 16

Occupations 45

People 45
Placenames 39
Political Correctness 33
Pronunciation 37
Pubs 104, 110

Queues 74

Received Pronunciation .. 30, 187
Registers 17
Rhyming Slang 65-70
Royalty .... (see Titles)
Rugby League 138
Rugby Union 135
Internationals 136

Shakespeare 20, 158
Shopping 111
Slang 223
Slang 49
Society 147
Spelling 27
Sport 125
Cricket 138
Football 125
Other Sports 143
Rugby League 138
Rugby Union 135
Structure, Language 23
Phrasal Verbs 26
Prefixes 25
Suffixes 25
Synonyms 24

Telephone Talk 47
Theatre 116
Titles 156
Forms of Address 156
Peers 157

Whisky 102
Wordplay 20
Words, Recycled 14

SCOTTISH GAELIC.. 229

Around Town 252
Dates 258
Drinks 257
Festivals 259
Food 256
Going Out........................... 251
Goodbyes 246
Grammar 236
  Adjectives 239
  Articles 237
  Demonstratives 241
  Have 242
  Know 244
  Negatives 244
  Nouns 236
  Past Tense 242
  Plurals 237
  Possession 238-239
  Present Tense 241
  Pronouns.......................... 240
  Questions 245

Verbs 241
  Word Order 236
  Yes & No 244
Greetings 246
Insults 243
Introduction 229
Language Difficulties 251
Making Conversation 248
Meeting People 245
Months 258
Numbers 261
Placenames 254
Pronunciation 233
  Consonants 234
  Vowels 233
Seasons 248
Signs 253
Time 258
Transliterations..............231-233
Well Wishes 250

SUGGESTED READING 291

Academic 295
General 293

Region 294

WELSH 263

Consonants 265
  Diphthongs 265
  Sound Changes 266
  Vowels 264
Dates 286
Days 286
Drinks 283

Family............................... 278
Festivals 286
Food 283
  Eating Out 283
  Traditional Dishes 284
Going Out........................... 280
Goodbyes 273

Graffiti 277
Grammar 266
  Adjectives 268
  Articles 266
  Be 271-272
  Nouns 267
  Plurals 267
  Prepositions 272
  Pronouns 269
  Verbs 270-272
  Word Order 266
Greetings 273

Insults 281
Interests 279
Introduction 263

Language Difficulties 278
Meeting People 273
Months 287
Nationalities 275
Nicknames 267
Numbers 288
Occupations 276
Placenames 285
Pronunciation 264
Pubs 285
Time 286
Transliterations 231-233
Unique Expressions 282
Well Wishes 274

Phrasebooks

L onely Planet phrasebooks are packed with essential words and phrases to help travellers communicate with the locals. With colour tabs for quick reference, an extensive vocabulary and use of script, these handy pocket-sized language guides cover day-to-day travel situations.

- handy pocket-sized books
- easy to understand Pronunciation chapter
- clear & comprehensive Grammar chapter
- romanisation alongside script to allow ease of pronunciation
- script throughout so users can point to phrases for every situation
- full of cultural information and tips for the traveller

'... vital for a real DIY spirit and attitude in language learning'
– Backpacker
'the phrasebooks have good cultural backgrounders and offer solid advice for challenging situations in remote locations'
– San Francisco Examiner

Australian *(Australian English, Aboriginal & Torres Strait languages)* • Baltic *(Estonian, Latvian, Lithuanian)* • Bengali • Brazilian • British *(English, dialects, Scottish Gaelic, Welsh)* • Burmese • Cantonese • Central Asia *(Kazakh, Kyrgyz, Pashto, Tajik, Tashkorghani, Turkmen, Uyghur, Uzbek & others)* • Central Europe *(Czech, German, Hungarian, Polish, Slovak, Slovene)* • Costa Rica Spanish • Czech • Eastern Europe *(Albanian, Bulgarian, Croatian, Czech, Hungarian, Macedonian, Polish, Romanian, Serbian, Slovak, Slovene)* • East Timor *(Tetun, Portuguese)* • Egyptian Arabic • Ethiopian (Amharic) • Europe *(Basque, Catalan, Dutch, French, German, Greek, Irish, Italian, Maltese, Portuguese, Scottish Gaelic, Spanish, Turkish, Welsh)* • Farsi (Persian) • Fijian • French • German • Greek • Hebrew • Hill Tribes *(Lahu, Akha, Lisu, Mong, Mien & others)* • Hindi & Urdu • Indonesian • Italian • Japanese • Korean • Lao • Latin American Spanish • Malay • Mandarin • Mongolian • Moroccan Arabic • Nepali • Pidgin • Pilipino (Tagalog) • Polish • Portuguese • Quechua • Russian • Scandinavian *(Danish, Faroese, Finnish, Icelandic, Norwegian, Swedish)* • South-East Asia *(Burmese, Indonesian, Khmer, Lao, Malay, Pilipino (Tagalog), Thai, Vietnamese)* • South Pacific *(Fijian, Hawaiian, Kanak languages, Maori, Niuean, Rapanui, Rarotongan Maori, Samoan, Tahitian, Tongan & others)* • Spanish *(Castilian, also includes Catalan, Galician & Basque)* • Sinhala • Swahili • Thai • Tibetan • Turkish • Ukrainian • USA *(US English, vernacular, Native American, Hawaiian)* • Vietnamese

COMPLETE LIST OF LONELY PLANET BOOKS

AFRICA Africa on a shoestring • Cairo • Cape Town • East Africa • Egypt • Ethiopia, Eritrea & Djibouti • The Gambia & Senegal • Healthy Travel Africa • Kenya • Malawi • Morocco • Mozambique • Read This First: Africa • South Africa, Lesotho & Swaziland • Southern Africa • Southern Africa Road Atlas • Tanzania, Zanzibar & Pemba • Trekking in East Africa • Tunisia • Watching Wildlife East Africa • Watching Wildlife Southern Africa • West Africa • World Food Morocco • Zimbabwe, Botswana & Namibia

AUSTRALIA & THE PACIFIC Aboriginal Australia & the Torres Strait Islands • Auckland • Australia • Australia Road Atlas • Bushwalking in Australia • Cycling Australia • Cycling New Zealand • Fiji • Healthy Travel Australia, NZ and the Pacific • Islands of Australia's Great Barrier Reef • Melbourne • Micronesia • New Caledonia • New South Wales & the ACT • New Zealand • Northern Territory • Outback Australia • Out to Eat – Melbourne • Out to Eat – Sydney • Papua New Guinea • Queensland • Rarotonga & the Cook Islands • Samoa • Solomon Islands • South Australia • South Pacific • Sydney • Sydney Condensed • Tahiti & French Polynesia • Tasmania • Tonga • Tramping in New Zealand • Vanuatu • Victoria • Walking in Australia • Watching Wildlife Australia • Western Australia

CENTRAL AMERICA & THE CARIBBEAN Bahamas, Turks & Caicos • Baja California • Bermuda • Central America on a shoestring • Costa Rica • Cuba • Dominican Republic & Haiti • Eastern Caribbean • Guatemala • Guatemala, Belize & Yucatán: La Ruta Maya • Havana • Healthy Travel Central & South America • Jamaica • Mexico • Mexico City • Panama • Puerto Rico • Read This First: Central & South America • World Food Mexico • Yucatán

EUROPE Amsterdam • Amsterdam Condensed • Andalucía • Austria • Barcelona • Belgium & Luxembourg • Berlin • Britain • Brussels, Bruges & Antwerp • Budapest • Canary Islands • Central Europe •Copenhagen • Corfu & the Ionians • Corsica • Crete • Crete Condensed • Croatia • Cycling Britain • Cycling France • Cyprus • Czech & Slovak Republics • Denmark • Dublin • Eastern Europe • Edinburgh • England • Estonia, Latvia & Lithuania • Europe on a shoestring • Finland • Florence • France • Frankfurt Condensed • Georgia, Armenia & Azerbaijan • Germany • Greece • Greek Islands • Hungary • Iceland, Greenland & the Faroe Islands • Ireland • Istanbul • Italy • Krakow • Lisbon • The Loire • London • London Condensed • Madrid • Malta • Mediterranean Europe • Milan, Turin & Genoa • Moscow • Mozambique • Munich • The Netherlands • Normandy • Norway • Out to Eat – London • Paris • Paris Condensed • Poland • Portugal • Prague • Provence & the Côte d'Azur • Read This First: Europe • Rhodes & the Dodecanese • Romania & Moldova • Rome • Rome Condensed • Russia, Ukraine & Belarus • Scandinavian & Baltic Europe • Scotland • Sicily • Slovenia • South-West France • Spain • St Petersburg • Sweden • Switzerland • Trekking in Spain • Tuscany • Venice • Vienna • Walking in Britain • Walking in France • Walking in Ireland • Walking in Italy • Walking in Spain • Walking in Switzerland • Western Europe • World Food France • World Food Ireland • World Food Italy • World Food Spain

COMPLETE LIST OF LONELY PLANET BOOKS

INDIAN SUBCONTINENT Bangladesh • Bhutan • Delhi • Goa • Healthy Travel Asia & India • India • Indian Himalaya • Karakoram Highway • Kerala • Mumbai (Bombay) • Nepal • Pakistan • Rajasthan • Read This First: Asia & India • South India • Sri Lanka • Tibet • Trekking in the Indian Himalaya • Trekking in the Karakoram & Hindukush • Trekking in the Nepal Himalaya

ISLANDS OF THE INDIAN OCEAN Madagascar &Comoros • Maldives • Mauritius, Réunion & Seychelles

MIDDLE EAST & CENTRAL ASIA Bahrain, Kuwait & Qatar • Central Asia • Dubai • Iran • Israel & the Palestinian Territories • Istanbul • Istanbul to Cairo on a Shoestring • Istanbul to Kathmandu • Jerusalem • Jordan • Lebanon • Middle East • Oman & the United Arab Emirates • Syria • Turkey • World Food Turkey • Yemen

NORTH AMERICA Alaska • Boston • Boston Condensed • British Colombia • California & Nevada • California Condensed • Canada • Chicago • Deep South • Florida • Great Lakes • Hawaii • Hiking in Alaska • Hiking in the USA • Honolulu • Las Vegas • Los Angeles • Louisiana & The Deep South • Miami • Montreal • New England • New Orleans • New York City • New York City Condensed • New York, New Jersey & Pennsylvania • Oahu • Out to Eat – San Francisco • Pacific Northwest • Puerto Rico • Rocky Mountains • San Francisco • San Francisco Map • Seattle • Southwest • Texas • Toronto • USA • Vancouver • Virginia & the Capital Region • Washington DC • World Food Deep South, USA • World Food New Orleans

NORTH-EAST ASIA Beijing • China • Hiking in Japan • Hong Kong • Hong Kong Condensed • Hong Kong, Macau & Guangzhou • Japan • Korea • Kyoto • Mongolia • Seoul • Shanghai • South-West China • Taiwan • Tokyo • World Food – Hong Kong

SOUTH AMERICA Argentina, Uruguay & Paraguay • Bolivia • Brazil • Buenos Aires • Chile & Easter Island • Colombia • Ecuador & the Galapagos Islands • Healthy Travel Central & South America • Peru • Read This First: Central & South America • Rio de Janeiro • Santiago • South America on a shoestring • Santiago • Trekking in the Patagonian Andes • Venezuela

SOUTH-EAST ASIA Bali & Lombok • Bangkok • Cambodia • Hanoi • Healthy Travel Asia & India • Ho Chi Minh City • Indonesia • Indonesia's Eastern Islands • Jakarta • Java • Laos • Malaysia, Singapore & Brunei • Myanmar (Burma) • Philippines • Read This First: Asia & India • Singapore • South-East Asia on a shoestring • Thailand • Thailand's Islands & Beaches • Thailand, Vietnam, Laos & Cambodia Road Atlas • Vietnam • World Food Thailand • World Food Vietnam

Also available; Journeys travel literature, illustrated pictorials, calendars, diaries, Lonely Planet maps and videos. For more information on these series and for the complete range of Lonely Planet products and services, visit our website at **www.lonelyplanet.com.**